marie claire
fresh + fast

marie claire
fresh + fast

SIMPLY DELICIOUS HEALTHY FOOD

Michele Cranston

MURDOCH BOOKS

contents

Food is all about life and living.

It's enriching, it's nourishing and it's the focus of a social activity that should be shared with family and friends as often as possible. It's hard to imagine a life that isn't about the sweet moments gathered around a table talking and laughing.

Food is the means by which we celebrate the beginning, middle and end of the day—but that doesn't mean its preparation should take up the hours in between! Food should be fun and fresh and with this in mind, I've written a book that is all about celebrating great ingredients cooked with simplicity.

Using fresh food is not only the simplest way to cook; it's also the most exciting and the best for you. Investing in excellent ingredients means that half the work is done. Good quality fresh food is just bursting with vitamins and flavour rather than hidden sugars and salts; so not only does it taste great but it's also good for you.

Whether you're putting together a quick mid-week meal or planning a leisurely dinner for friends, these recipes are full of ideas that help make it easy: leafy greens with a splash of dressing, rosy tomatoes with a sprinkle of sea salt, jewel-toned beetroot richly baked, tangy fruit with a spiced sweetness and silvery seafoods grilled with a citrus zest.

It's as simple as that. With the addition of a few store cupboard essentials, a little bit of work with a knife, spoon and bowl and a dash of imagination there is no excuse not to eat well.

So zip into the kitchen and bake, slice and bite your way into comforting, sweet fun. Or simply pile some fabulous ingredients into a bowl and share the goodness.

fresh

flavours, easy meals

WATERMELON AND FETA SALAD
ZUCCHINI, TOMATO AND BOCCONCINI SALAD
CHICKEN AND PAPAYA SALAD
FRESH TOMATO AND ROCKET PASTA
SWEET CARROT AND PARSLEY SOUP
WITLOF AND CELERY SALAD WITH BOILED EGGS
CARROT, ORANGE AND GINGER SALAD
ORANGE AND WATERCRESS SALAD
POACHED CHICKEN WITH HERBED TOMATO SAUCE
PAN-FRIED HALOUMI WITH ROASTED TOMATOES

watermelon and feta salad

750 g (1 lb 10 oz) seedless watermelon
200 g (7 oz/1½ cups) Bulgarian feta cheese
20 kalamata olives, pitted and finely sliced
12 mint leaves, finely sliced
2 celery stalks, finely sliced
1 tablespoon red wine vinegar
2 tablespoons olive oil

Remove the rind from the watermelon, then cut the flesh into bite-sized pieces. Cut the feta into 2 cm cubes. Roughly pile the watermelon and feta onto a serving platter, then scatter with the olives, mint and celery.

Combine the vinegar and olive oil in a small bowl and drizzle over the salad. Season lightly with freshly ground black pepper.

SERVES 4

zucchini, tomato and bocconcini salad

4 zucchini (courgettes)
1 teaspoon sea salt
2 ripe tomatoes
8 baby bocconcini cheeses
2 basil leaves
4 tablespoons olive oil
1 tablespoon apple cider vinegar

Using a vegetable peeler, peel the flesh of the zucchini to form ribbons. Put these in a bowl, sprinkle with the sea salt and toss several times to ensure the zucchini is well coated. Allow to sit for 10 minutes.

Meanwhile, finely chop the tomatoes and cut the baby bocconcinis in half.

Drain any excess liquid from the zucchini and pat dry on paper towel before arranging on a serving platter. Top with the tomatoes and bocconcini. Thinly slice the basil leaves and scatter over the salad.

In a small bowl whisk together the olive oil and vinegar, then spoon this dressing over the salad. Season with freshly ground black pepper. Serve with crusty bread.

SERVES 4

chicken and papaya salad

1 tablespoon tamarind pulp
1 teaspoon soy sauce
2 teaspoons finely grated fresh ginger
1 tablespoon grated palm sugar (jaggery)
½ teaspoon ground cumin
1 large red chilli, seeded and finely sliced
350 g (12 oz/2 cups) shredded roast chicken meat
40 g (1½ oz) English spinach leaves
1 red papaya, peeled and seeded
80 g (2¾ oz/½ cup) peanuts, roughly chopped
1 Lebanese (short) cucumber, diced
2 tablespoons Asian fried onions
2 spring onions (scallions), finely sliced on the diagonal
a handful of mint leaves

Mix the tamarind with 3 tablespoons of water, then add the soy sauce, ginger, palm sugar, cumin and chilli. Stir until the sugar has dissolved. Add the chicken to the dressing and toss together.

Arrange the spinach leaves on a serving platter. Top with bite-sized chunks of papaya, then scatter with the peanuts, cucumber, fried onions and spring onion. Arrange the dressed chicken over the top of the salad, then scatter with the mint leaves. Drizzle any remaining dressing over the top.

SERVES 4

fresh tomato and rocket pasta

4 large ripe tomatoes
1 heaped teaspoon sea salt
2 tablespoons small salted capers, rinsed and drained
15 basil leaves, finely chopped
a handful of flat-leaf (Italian) parsley, roughly chopped
350 g (12 oz) orechiette
75 g (2½ oz/¾ cup) finely grated parmesan cheese
2 handfuls of baby rocket (arugula) leaves
3 tablespoons extra virgin olive oil

Chop the tomatoes and put them in a bowl with the sea salt, capers, basil and parsley. Stir gently to coat all the tomato, then set aside.

Bring a large pot of salted water to the boil, add the pasta and cook until *al dente*. Drain and return to the warm pot.

Add the parmesan, rocket and olive oil to the pasta, stir a few times, then add the tomato mixture. Season with freshly ground black pepper, toss together well and spoon into four warm pasta bowls. Serve immediately.

SERVES 4

sweet carrot and parsley soup

1 litre (35 fl oz/4 cups) chicken stock
100g (3½ oz/1 bunch) parsley, rinsed
50 g (1¾ oz) butter
2 garlic cloves, crushed
2 onions, finely diced
400 g (14 oz/2½ cups) carrots, peeled and finely diced

Put the chicken stock in a saucepan over a medium heat. Finely chop 2 tablespoons of the parsley and set to one side. Add the remainder of the bunch to the stock.

In another saucepan put the butter, garlic and onion and sauté over a medium heat until the onion is soft and transparent. Add the carrots and cook for 5 minutes, stirring occasionally, before adding the stock. Remove and discard the parsley. Cook the soup for 40 minutes or until the carrot is soft, then remove from the heat.

Blend to a smooth purée, then return the soup to the saucepan over a low heat. Season to taste with sea salt and white pepper and add the chopped parsley.

SERVES 4

witlof and celery salad with boiled eggs

witlof and celery salad with boiled eggs

4 organic eggs at room temperature
2 witlof (chicory/Belgian endive),
    finely sliced
2 celery stalks, finely sliced
2 tablespoons finely chopped parsley
1 teaspoon cider vinegar
2 tablespoons extra virgin olive oil
2 tablespoons good quality
    mayonnaise

Bring a pot of water to the boil and add the eggs. Boil for 5 minutes, then remove and allow to cool. Peel the eggs.

Put the witlof and celery in a serving bowl. Roughly chop the eggs and add them to the salad, then sprinkle with the chopped parsley.

In a small bowl, stir together the vinegar and olive oil and spoon over the salad, before adding dollops of mayonnaise.

SERVES 4

carrot, orange and ginger salad

1 teaspoon finely grated fresh ginger
1 tablespoon maple syrup
2 tablespoons olive oil
2 tablespoons orange juice
3 carrots
3 handfuls of picked watercress sprigs
40 g (1½ oz/⅓ cup) shelled unsalted
    pistachios

Put the ginger, maple syrup, olive oil and orange juice in a small bowl, then season lightly with sea salt and freshly ground black pepper. Stir until well combined.

Grate the carrot and put it into a bowl. Drizzle with the dressing and toss to ensure the carrot is well coated. Arrange the dressed carrot on a serving plate with the watercress and a sprinkle of pistachio nuts. Serve with grilled fish or chicken.

SERVES 4

orange and watercress salad

1 red onion, finely sliced
1 tablespoon sea salt
1 tablespoon lemon juice
3 handfuls of picked watercress sprigs
4 oranges

Put the finely sliced onion in a bowl and sprinkle with a tablespoon of sea salt. Toss to ensure the onion is well coated in the salt. Allow to sit for 10 minutes, then lightly rinse under cold running water. Squeeze to remove any excess liquid and put in a small bowl with the lemon juice.

Arrange the watercress on a serving plate. Slice away the skin and pith of the oranges. Holding the oranges over the watercress, remove the orange segments by running a sharp knife between the individual membranes, then arrange the segments on the watercress. Allow any excess juice to drizzle over the salad. Top with the onion and serve.

SERVES 4

poached chicken with herbed tomato sauce

1 heaped tablespoon sea salt
4 small chicken breasts
a generous handful of flat-leaf (Italian) parsley leaves
12 large mint leaves
2 tablespoons finely chopped preserved lemon rind
2 ripe tomatoes, finely chopped
4 tablespoons extra virgin olive oil
300 g (10½ oz) green beans, trimmed

Put the sea salt in a large pot of water and bring to the boil. When the water is boiling, add the chicken breasts, cover with a tight-fitting lid and remove from the heat. Leave covered for half an hour.

Roughly chop the parsley and mint, then put them in a small bowl with the preserved lemon, tomato and extra virgin olive oil. Allow to sit for 10 minutes while the chicken is poaching.

Bring a small pot of water to the boil and blanch the beans until emerald green. Drain and divide among four serving plates. Remove the poached chicken and thickly slice against the grain. Arrange over the top of the beans, then spoon over the herbed tomato sauce.

SERVES 4

pan-fried haloumi with roasted tomatoes

2 branches of truss cherry tomatoes
2 tablespoons olive oil
400 g (14 oz) tinned white beans, drained
2 small zucchini (courgettes), finely sliced
a handful of parsley leaves
2 handfuls of rocket (arugula) leaves
2 tablespoons lemon juice
2 tablespoons extra virgin olive oil
250 g (9 oz) haloumi cheese, sliced

Preheat the oven to 200°C (400°F/Gas 6).

Cut the truss tomato branches into two so that you have four sections of tomatoes.
Place them onto a baking tray and drizzle with 1 tablespoon of olive oil. Bake in the oven
for 10 minutes or until the skins are beginning to split.

Put the white beans in a bowl with the zucchini, parsley leaves, rocket leaves, lemon juice
and extra virgin olive oil. Season with sea salt and freshly ground black pepper. Toss to
combine before dividing between four serving plates.

Heat a non-stick frying pan over a medium heat and add the remaining olive oil. Pan-fry the
haloumi slices until golden brown on both sides. Arrange the haloumi slices over the salad
and top with the baked tomatoes.

SERVES 4

fast

delicious and now

CINNAMON RICOTTA WITH NECTARINES AND HONEY
BOILED EGG WITH SPICES   PROSCIUTTO AND PAPAYA SALAD
TOMATO SALAD WITH CORIANDER AND CHILLI SALSA
HAM SALAD WITH PEACH AND PECAN
OMELETTE WITH JULIENNED VEGETABLES
SMOKED SALMON WITH CUCUMBER   RISONI WITH PESTO AND TUNA
WITLOF AND AVOCADO SALAD

cinnamon ricotta with nectarines and honey

200 g (7 oz/1 cup) ricotta cheese
200 g (7 oz/1 cup) Greek-style yoghurt
½ teaspoon ground cinnamon
4 ripe nectarines, quartered
2 tablespoons honey

Put the ricotta in a bowl and add half the yoghurt and the cinnamon. Stir until well combined, then add the remaining yoghurt, folding it through until it gives a slightly marbled effect. Dollop onto four serving plates, then add the nectarine quarters.

Drizzle with honey and serve.

SERVES 4

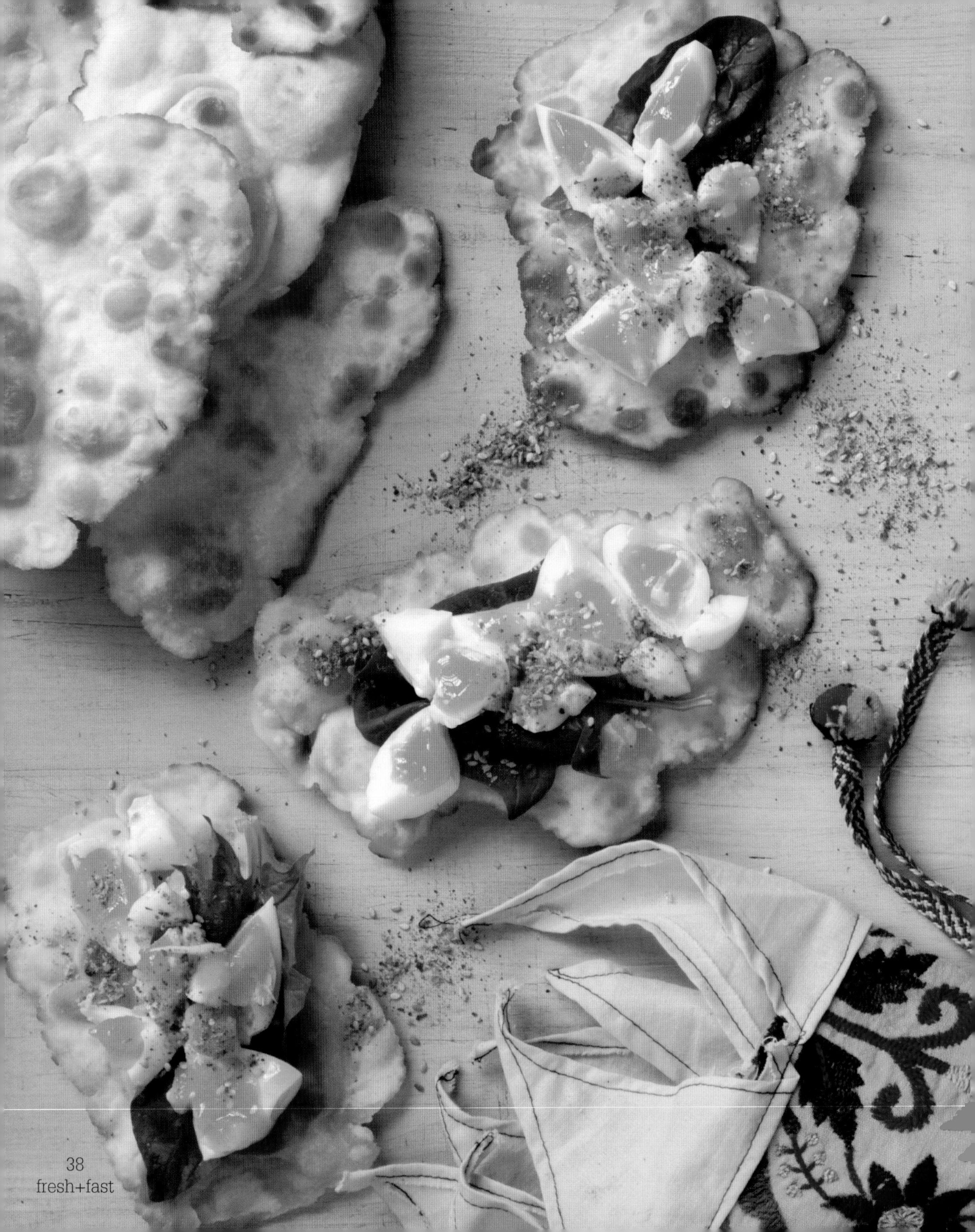

boiled egg with spices

1 tablespoon sea salt
½ teaspoon ground turmeric
1 tablespoon toasted sesame seeds
1 teaspoon ground cumin
1 teaspoon sumac
4 organic eggs at room temperature
a handful of baby English spinach
    leaves
4 pieces pide (Turkish/flat bread)
2 teaspoons butter

Combine the salt, turmeric, sesame seeds,
cumin and sumac in a small bowl and set
to one side.

Bring a saucepan of water to the boil and
add the eggs. Boil the eggs for 5 minutes,
then lift them out of the water and leave to
cool. When they are cool enough to handle,
peel the eggs.

Divide the spinach leaves among the
four pieces of bread and top with the
warm peeled eggs. Roughly chop the
eggs, dab with butter and sprinkle with
the seasoned salt.

SERVES 4

prosciutto and papaya salad

prosciutto and papaya salad

1 orange, juiced
1 teaspoon red wine vinegar
3 tablespoons extra virgin olive oil
2 small red papayas
8 slices prosciutto
15 small basil leaves

Put the orange juice, vinegar and olive oil in a small bowl and mix together to make a dressing.

Cut each papaya into quarters, then remove the seeds and skin. Cut the flesh into small wedges and arrange on a serving platter. Tear the prosciutto into bite-sized bits and toss them over the papaya. Scatter the basil leaves over the top.

Stir the dressing again, drizzle it over the salad and sprinkle with freshly ground black pepper.

SERVES 4

tomato salad with coriander and chilli salsa

4 large ripe tomatoes
a handful of mixed fresh herb leaves
1 red onion, finely diced
2 large red chillies, seeded and finely chopped
3 tablespoons extra virgin olive oil
1 tablespoon balsamic vinegar

Thickly slice the tomatoes and arrange them on a serving platter. Scatter with the mixed herb leaves, onion and chillies. Season with sea salt and freshly ground black pepper.

Put the olive oil and vinegar in a small bowl and whisk to combine. Drizzle the dressing over the salad.

SERVES 4

ham salad with peach and pecan

4 small ripe peaches
2 tablespoons extra virgin olive oil
1 tablespoon balsamic vinegar
1 buffalo mozzarella cheese
100 g (3½ oz/2¼ cups) baby rocket (arugula) leaves
250 g (9 oz) leg ham, finely sliced off the bone
40 g (1½ oz/⅓ cup) pecans, roughly chopped

Halve the peaches and remove the skin before slicing them into a bowl. Add the olive oil and balsamic vinegar, and toss to combine. Season lightly with sea salt and freshly ground black pepper.

Tear the mozzarella into bite-sized pieces. Arrange the rocket on a serving platter and top with the leg ham and mozzarella. Add the peaches and pecans and drizzle with any remaining dressing.

SERVES 4

omelette with julienned vegetables

4 asparagus spears
½ small red capsicum (pepper)
½ small zucchini (courgette)
3 eggs, separated
1 tablespoon butter
12 small basil leaves
30 g (1 oz/¼ cup) cheddar cheese, grated

Bring a small saucepan of water to the boil. Cut the asparagus spears in half lengthways, then cut in half again. Blanch the spears in the boiling water for a minute, then drain and refresh under cold running water. Put the cooked asparagus into a bowl. Finely julienne the capsicum and zucchini and add to the bowl.

In a clean bowl whisk the egg whites until they form soft peaks. Heat the butter in a large non-stick frying pan over a medium heat, then fold the egg yolks through the egg whites. Pour the egg mixture into the pan and cook for a few minutes or until the base of the omelette is golden brown and firm.

Arrange the mixed vegetables and basil leaves over one side of the omelette and scatter with grated cheese. Gently lift up the other side of the omelette and flip it over the vegetables. Place the pan under a hot grill (broiler) until the omelette is cooked and the cheese is bubbling.

Remove from the heat. Divide into two and gently lift onto two serving plates.

SERVES 2

smoked salmon with cucumber

1 telegraph (long) cucumber
1 teaspoon sea salt
1 tablespoon lemon juice
1 teaspoon finely chopped dill
100 g (3½ oz) light sour cream
black pepper
12 slices smoked salmon

Peel the whole cucumber, then cut it in half lengthways. Use a teaspoon to scrape away the seeds, then finely slice the cucumber. Put it in a bowl with a teaspoon of sea salt and toss lightly. Leave to sit for 10 minutes. Squeeze any of the excess juice from the cucumber, then add the lemon juice and dill.

Put the sour cream into a small bowl and stir in a generous grind of black pepper.

Divide the salmon among four plates, then top with the cucumber and a dollop of sour cream. Season with freshly ground black pepper.

SERVES 4

risoni with pesto and tuna

100 g (3½ oz) risoni
250 g (9 oz) tinned Italian-style tuna,
   drained
3 tablespoons pesto sauce (see Store,
   page 242)
100 g (3½ oz/3 cups) rocket (arugula)
   leaves
1 tablespoon lemon juice

Bring a pot of salted water to the boil.
Cook the risoni until *al dente*, then remove
and drain. Put the pasta in a large serving
bowl and add the tuna, pesto, rocket and
lemon juice. Toss to combine, and season
to taste with sea salt and freshly ground
black pepper.

SERVES 4

witlof and avocado salad

2 witlof (chicory/Belgian endive)
2 ripe avocados
10 mint leaves
2 pink grapefruit
2 tablespoons extra virgin olive oil

Cut the witlof lengthways into eighths and
put in a serving bowl. Cut the avocados in
half and remove the stones. Slice the flesh
into bite-sized chunks, then remove with
a large spoon and add to the bowl. Tear
the mint leaves and scatter over the salad.

With a sharp knife remove the skin and
pith from the two grapefruit. Remove the
segments by running a sharp knife
between the individual membranes (do
this over the salad so that the juice runs
over the witlof and avocado). Arrange the
grapefruit segments on top of the salad.
Drizzle with the extra virgin olive oil and
season with sea salt and freshly ground
black pepper.

SERVES 4

leafy greens

cooked or raw

BUTTER LETTUCE, GREEN PEA AND RICOTTA
SPINACH SALAD WITH GRATED EGG AND PROSCIUTTO
TOMATO AND BREAD SALAD
ASPARAGUS AND COS SALAD WITH SMOKED TROUT
ROCKET AND PEAR SALAD
PRAWN AND SNOW PEA SPROUT SALAD WITH CHILLI SAUCE
PEA AND LETTUCE SOUP
SILVERBEET AND POTATO SOUP
NICOISE SALAD
WATERCRESS SALAD WITH SMOKED SALMON

butter lettuce, green pea and ricotta

butter lettuce, green pea and ricotta

150 g (5½ oz/1 cup) frozen green peas
100 g (3½ oz/1 cup) sugarsnap peas, trimmed
100 g (3½ oz/1 cup) snow peas (mangetout), trimmed
1 tablespoon lemon juice
2 tablespoons extra virgin olive oil
1 butter lettuce, rinsed
200 g (7 oz/1 cup) ricotta cheese

Bring a saucepan of salted water to the boil and cook the frozen peas for 10 minutes. Add the sugarsnaps and snow peas and cook for a further few minutes until they are emerald green. Drain, then rinse under cold running water. Put the peas in a bowl and add the lemon juice and olive oil. Season with sea salt and freshly ground black pepper.

Arrange the lettuce leaves on a serving platter, then spoon over the peas. Add the ricotta in rough spoonfuls all over the salad and drizzle with any remaining dressing.

SERVES 4

spinach salad with grated egg and prosciutto

1 bunch English spinach
4 hard-boiled eggs
4 slices prosciutto
1 tablespoon apple cider vinegar
3 tablespoons extra virgin olive oil
2 tablespoons finely chopped parsley

Rinse and dry the spinach leaves.

Finely slice the leaves and divide among
four serving bowls. Grate one egg over
each salad and season lightly with sea salt
and freshly ground black pepper.

Heat a non-stick frying pan over a medium
heat and fry the prosciutto until crisp.
Drain on paper towel, then crumble over
the top of the salad.

Whisk together the vinegar and olive oil
and lightly drizzle over the salad before
sprinkling with the chopped parsley.

SERVES 4

left: tomato and bread salad
right: asparagus and cos salad with smoked trout

tomato and bread salad

400 g (14 oz) ripe tomatoes
2 teaspoons sea salt
2 tablespoons extra virgin olive oil
4 basil leaves, shredded
¼ red onion, finely sliced
100 g (3½ oz) stale sourdough
80 g (2¾ oz) baby rocket (arugula)
   leaves

Roughly chop the tomatoes and put
them in a large bowl with the salt and
olive oil. Add the basil leaves and onion
and toss to combine. Tear the sourdough
into small bite-sized pieces, add to the
salad and toss.

Arrange the rocket on a serving platter,
then top with the tomato and bread salad.

SERVES 4

asparagus and cos salad with smoked trout

12 asparagus spears, trimmed
1 small cos (romaine) lettuce, rinsed
a handful of flat-leaf (Italian)
   parsley leaves
1 celery stalk, finely sliced
4 radishes, finely sliced
1 spring onion (scallion), finely sliced
400 g (14 oz) smoked trout
lemon mayonnaise (see Store,
   page 241)

Bring a pot of salted water to the boil and
blanch the asparagus until it is emerald
green. Drain, then rinse under cold
running water. Cut the spears in half.

Slice the cos into thick strips and put
on a serving platter. Add the asparagus
pieces, parsley leaves, celery, radish and
spring onion. Break the smoked trout
into bite-sized pieces and arrange over
the salad. Drizzle with the lemon
mayonnaise and season with freshly
ground black pepper.

SERVES 4

rocket and pear salad

1 teaspoon white wine vinegar
1 teaspoon dijon mustard
½ teaspoon honey
2 tablespoons olive oil
200 g (7 oz) baby rocket (arugula)
    leaves
2 beurre bosc pears, thinly sliced
100 g (3½ oz/1 cup) parmesan
    cheese, shaved

In a small bowl, whisk together the
vinegar, mustard and honey. While still
whisking, slowly add the olive oil, then
season with sea salt and freshly ground
black pepper.

Arrange the rocket leaves, pear slices and
parmesan in a serving bowl and drizzle
with the dressing.

SERVES 4

prawn and snow pea sprout salad with chilli sauce

2 whole coriander (cilantro) stems
1 garlic clove
sea salt
1 small red chilli
3 tablespoons palm sugar (jaggery)
2 tablespoons fish sauce
3 tablespoons lime juice
40 g (1½ oz) snow pea (mangetout) sprouts, trimmed of stalks
1 spring onion (scallion), finely sliced on the diagonal
1 red capsicum (pepper), julienned
1 Lebanese (short) cucumber, diced
16 raw king prawns, peeled and deveined

Remove the stems and root from the coriander and wash. Dry with paper towel. Set the leaves aside. Using a mortar and pestle pound the garlic and coriander stems and roots with a sprinkle of sea salt until roughly mashed, then add the chilli and grind to a fine paste. Spoon into a small bowl and add the palm sugar, fish sauce and lime juice. Stir until the sugar has dissolved, then set to one side.

Arrange the snow pea sprouts, spring onion, capsicum and cucumber on four plates.

Heat a non-stick frying pan over a medium to high heat and sear the prawns on both sides until pink and curled. Remove and divide the prawns among the four plates. Drizzle with the dressing and scatter with the coriander leaves.

SERVES 4

pea and lettuce soup

2 tablespoons olive oil
1 leek, finely sliced
1 garlic clove, crushed
1.5 litres (52 fl oz/6 cups) vegetable or
   chicken stock
2 butter lettuces, stems removed,
   finely sliced
300 g (10½ oz/2 cups) frozen peas
1 teaspoon sugar
20 mint leaves
finely grated parmesan cheese,
   to serve

Put the olive oil, leek and garlic into a large
saucepan and sauté over a medium heat
until the leek is soft. Add the stock, lettuce
and peas and bring to the boil. Reduce
the heat and simmer for 15 minutes, or
until the peas are soft, then remove the
pan from the heat and add the sugar and
mint leaves.

Pour the soup mixture into a blender or
food processor and blend until it is
smooth. Season well with sea salt and
ground black pepper.

Serve the soup with some grated parmesan
to sprinkle over.

SERVES 4

silverbeet and potato soup

1 kg (2 lb 4 oz/1 bunch) silverbeet
   (Swiss chard)
30 g (1 oz) butter
1 leek, washed, trimmed and finely
   chopped
400 g (14 oz) desirée potatoes, peeled
   and diced
1.5 litres (52 fl oz/6 cups) chicken stock
¼ teaspoon ground nutmeg
goats curd or light sour cream to serve

Rinse the silverbeet under cold running
water and cut away the white stalks.
Roughly chop the green leaves.

Put the butter and chopped leek into a large
saucepan and sauté over a medium heat.
When the leek is soft and transparent add
the silverbeet and potatoes and stir for a
minute. Add the stock and nutmeg, then
allow to simmer for half an hour or until the
potatoes are cooked through. Allow to cool,
then blend to a smooth purée in a blender
or food processor.

Return to the saucepan and warm when
ready to serve. Serve with a dollop of goats
curd or light sour cream.

SERVES 4

niçoise salad

8 small waxy potatoes
150 g (5½ oz) green beans, trimmed
4 eggs
2 small butter lettuces
185 g (6½ oz) tinned Italian-style tuna
2 ripe tomatoes, cut into eighths
½ red onion, finely sliced
20 small black olives
1 tablespoon small salted capers, rinsed
a handful of flat-leaf (Italian) parsley leaves
2 tablespoons lemon juice
4 tablespoons extra virgin olive oil
¼ teaspoon crushed garlic
8 anchovies

Boil the potatoes until cooked through, then drain and cut in half. Blanch the beans in boiling water until emerald green, then drain and rinse. Boil the eggs for 5 minutes, then remove and allow to cool.

Divide the leaves of the butter lettuce among four bowls and top with the potatoes and beans. Shell the eggs and cut in half before adding to the salad. Drain the tuna and add to the bowls along with the tomato pieces and onion. Add a scattering of olives, capers and parsley leaves.

Combine the lemon juice, olive oil and garlic and drizzle over the salad. Garnish each salad with two anchovies.

SERVES 4

watercress salad with smoked salmon

2 tablespoons kecap manis
1 teaspoon balsamic vinegar
1 teaspoon finely grated fresh ginger
1 teaspoon sesame oil
200 g (7 oz) smoked salmon
60 g (2¼ oz/2 cups) picked watercress sprigs
4 red radishes, finely sliced
1 tablespoon toasted sesame seeds

Put the kecap manis, vinegar, ginger and sesame oil in a small bowl
and stir to combine.

Lay the smoked salmon on four serving plates, then top with
the watercress and radish slices. Drizzle with the dressing and
sprinkle with sesame seeds.

SERVES 4

splash

and salt, seafood to go

CRAB AND CHILLI PASTA
MUSSELS WITH ROUILLE AND HERB SALAD
SEARED TUNA WITH TOMATO, BASIL AND OLIVES
BAKED SCALLOPS WITH AVOCADO SALSA
BLUE EYE COD FILLETS WITH A MIXED BEAN SALAD
BAKED BLUE EYE COD WITH CHILLI SNAKE BEANS
GRILLED PRAWNS WITH PARSLEY AND CAPER SAUCE
WHITING FILLETS WRAPPED IN VINE LEAVES
SEARED TUNA WITH BUCKWHEAT NOODLES
SNAPPER WRAPPED IN FRESH HERBS
SALMON CEVICHE WITH LEMON CHERVIL DRESSING

crab and chilli pasta

350 g (12 oz) fresh crabmeat
2 large red chillies, seeded and finely chopped
grated zest and juice of 1 lemon
4 tablespoons extra virgin olive oil
a handful of flat-leaf (Italian) parsley, roughly chopped
150 g (5½ oz) baby rocket (arugula) leaves
300 g (10½ oz) linguini

Put the crabmeat in a large bowl and roughly flake it with a fork. Add the chilli, lemon zest, lemon juice and olive oil. Season liberally with sea salt and freshly ground black pepper. Stir to combine. Pile the parsley and rocket on top.

Bring a large pot of salted water to the boil and add the linguini. Cook until *al dente*, then drain and add to the crab mixture. Toss well until the rocket has wilted, then divide among four warmed pasta bowls.

SERVES 4

mussels with rouille and herb salad

2 kg (4 lb 8 oz) mussels
2 tablespoons olive oil
1 white onion, finely chopped
2 garlic cloves, crushed
400 g (14 oz) tinned tomatoes, roughly chopped
1 bay leaf
1 fennel bulb, finely diced
a pinch of saffron threads
250 ml (9 fl oz/1 cup) white wine
a handful of flat-leaf (Italian) parsley leaves
50 g (1¾ oz) baby leaf salad
rouille (see Store, page 242) or mayonnaise

Clean the mussels in the sink under cold running water, scrubbing them to remove any barnacles or bits of hairy 'beard'. Discard any that are open and that do not close when you tap them.

Put the olive oil, onion and garlic in a large lidded saucepan and cook them over a low heat until the onion is transparent. Add the tomatoes, bay leaf, fennel and saffron and simmer for 10 minutes. Season with 1 teaspoon of sea salt. Pour in the wine, bring the sauce to the boil and add the mussels. Cover with the lid and cook for a few minutes, shaking the pan once or twice, then check that all the mussels have opened. (Discard any unopened mussels.)

Divide the mussels among four big bowls, sprinkle with the parsley and salad leaves and dollop with rouille or mayonnaise.

SERVES 4

seared tuna with tomato, basil and olives

10 cherry tomatoes, halved
10 basil leaves, roughly torn
20 small black olives
2 tablespoons balsamic vinegar
4 tablespoons extra virgin olive oil
1 teaspoon olive oil
4 x 150 g (5½ oz) tuna fillets
150 g (5½ oz) rocket (arugula) leaves, stalks removed

Put the tomatoes, basil, olives, vinegar and extra virgin olive oil in a small bowl and toss together.

Put the olive oil in a frying pan over a high heat. Add the tuna and sear on one side for 1 minute. Turn the fillets over and reduce the heat to medium. Cook for a further 3 minutes.

Serve the tuna on warmed plates with some rocket leaves and top with the tomato and olive mixture.

SERVES 4

baked scallops with avocado salsa

baked scallops with avocado salsa

1 avocado, finely diced
2 tablespoons finely chopped coriander (cilantro) leaves
1 large red chilli, seeded and finely chopped
1 tablespoon lime juice
1 teaspoon light olive oil
16 scallops, cleaned and on the half shell
1 tablespoon softened butter

Preheat the oven to 200°C (400°F/Gas 6).

In a bowl, combine the avocado, coriander, chilli, lime juice and olive oil. Season lightly with sea salt and freshly ground black pepper. Set to one side.

Place the scallops on a baking tray and dab each one with a little butter. Bake in the oven for 2–3 minutes. Remove and arrange on a serving platter. Spoon over the salsa and serve.

SERVES 4

blue eye cod fillets with a mixed bean salad

120 g (4¼ oz) green beans, trimmed and cut into 4 cm lengths
120 g (4¼ oz) butterbeans (lima beans), trimmed
400 g (14 oz) tinned white beans, drained
1 tablespoon extra virgin olive oil
1 tablespoon lemon juice
1 tablespoon olive oil
4 x 200 g (7 oz) blue eye cod fillets
4 lemon wedges to serve

Bring a pot of salted water to the boil and add the beans and butterbeans. Cook until the green beans have turned emerald green, then drain. Put these beans in a bowl with the white beans, extra virgin olive oil and lemon juice.

Heat the olive oil in a non-stick frying pan over a high heat and add the blue eye cod fillets. Sear for 2 minutes on one side then turn over and cook for a further 2–3 minutes.

Divide the bean salad among four plates and top with the blue eye cod fillets. Serve with a wedge of lemon.

SERVES 4

baked blue eye cod with chilli snake beans

4 x 180 g (6¼ oz) blue eye cod fillets
1 large knob of fresh ginger, finely sliced
1 lemongrass stem, finely sliced
juice of 1 lemon
1 tablespoon butter
1 bunch snake (yard-long) beans
1 large red chilli, finely chopped
1 teaspoon olive oil
1 teaspoon sesame oil
2 tablespoons kecap manis

Preheat the oven to 180°C (350°F/Gas 4).

Rinse the fish fillets under cold running water, then dry with paper towel.

Take four large pieces of baking paper. Arrange the ginger and lemongrass slices in the centre of the paper, then top with the fish fillets. Spoon over the lemon juice and add a dab of butter, then season with sea salt and freshly ground black pepper. Wrap the fish fillets in the baking paper to form neat parcels. Put the parcels on an oven tray and bake for 20 minutes.

Trim the beans into 8 cm lengths and put them in a bowl with the chilli, olive oil and sesame oil. Toss until the beans are well coated in the oil.

Heat a wok over a high heat and add the beans. Stir fry for a few minutes, then add the kecap manis. Toss a few times, then remove to a serving plate. Serve with the baked fish fillets.

SERVES 4

grilled prawns with parsley
and caper sauce

grilled prawns with parsley and caper sauce

1 tablespoon salted capers, lightly rinsed
a handful of parsley leaves
3 tablespoons lemon juice
150 g (5½ oz/¾ cup) wild rice
4 tablespoons butter
20 raw king prawns, peeled and deveined
green salad to serve

In a small bowl combine the capers, parsley leaves and lemon juice. Set to one side.

Bring a pot of salted water to the boil and add the rice. Cook for 30 minutes or until tender, then drain. Return to the warm saucepan until ready to serve.

When the rice has 10 minutes remaining to cook, heat 1 tablespoon of butter and cook the prawns until pink and curled up. Depending on the size of the frying pan you may need to do this in several batches, storing the cooked prawns on a warm plate until ready to serve. When all the prawns have been cooked, spoon the warm rice onto four plates, then arrange the prawns on top.

Put the remaining butter in the pan. When it has melted and is beginning to bubble add the capers, parsley and lemon juice. Swirl to combine then spoon the buttery juice over the prawns and rice. Season with freshly ground black pepper and serve with a green salad.

SERVES 4

whiting fillets wrapped in vine leaves

8–12 vine leaves
8 large whiting fillets, deboned
1 tablespoon butter
4 basil leaves
1 ripe tomato, finely diced
1 Lebanese (short) cucumber, diced
a handful of flat-leaf (Italian) parsley
    leaves, roughly chopped
lemon wedges and extra virgin
    olive oil to serve

Preheat the oven to 180°C (350°/Gas 4).

On a clean board, arrange 2–3 of the vine leaves so that they slightly overlap. Place one of the whiting fillets skin side down in the centre of the leaves and spread a dab of butter over the flesh. Add one of the basil leaves and some of the tomato, then top with another fillet, this time flesh side down. Wrap the vine leaves into a neat bundle around the fillets, then place on a baking tray. Repeat with the remaining ingredients.

Bake the four fish parcels in the oven for 15 minutes. Remove and place on a warm serving platter. Open the leaves and scatter with the cucumber and parsley. Drizzle with a little extra virgin olive oil and season with freshly ground black pepper. Serve with lemon wedges on the side.

SERVES 4

seared tuna with buckwheat noodles

3 tablespoons soy sauce
3 tablespoons sesame oil
1½ tablespoons balsamic vinegar
3 tablespoons brown sugar
3 tablespoons lime juice
1 tablespoon finely chopped lemongrass
1 red chilli, seeded and finely chopped
1 teaspoon finely chopped fresh ginger
300 g (10½ oz) buckwheat noodles
a handful of mint leaves
a handful of coriander (cilantro) leaves
1 red capsicum (pepper), julienned
1 Lebanese (short) cucumber, julienned
1 tablespoon olive oil
4 x 100 g (3½ oz) tuna fillets

Put the soy sauce, sesame oil, vinegar, brown sugar, lime juice, lemongrass, chilli and ginger in a large bowl and stir until the sugar has dissolved. Set aside.

Bring a large pot of water to the boil and cook the noodles until *al dente*, then drain and rinse them under cold running water. Put them in the bowl with the dressing and add the mint, coriander, capsicum and cucumber. Toss to combine then pile into four pasta bowls.

Heat a non-stick frying pan over a high heat and add the olive oil. Sear the tuna fillets for 2 minutes on each side, and break into large chunks. Serve the tuna on top of the noodles.

SERVES 4

snapper wrapped in fresh herbs

4 small snappers, scaled and cleaned
150 g (5½ oz/1 bunch) flat-leaf
   (Italian) parsley
120 g (4¼ oz/1 bunch) basil
4 tablespoons extra virgin olive oil
1 lemon, cut into 8 slices
1 bunch dill
4 tablespoons butter
boiled new potatoes to serve

Preheat the oven to 180°C (350°F/Gas 4).

Rinse the snappers under cold running water, then pat dry with paper towel.

Arrange four large squares of baking paper on a clean surface. Put some of the parsley and basil sprigs on each of the squares and drizzle with a little of the olive oil. Lay each of the fish on top of the herbs. Divide the lemon slices among the fish and place them in the cavities. Top each fish with some of the dill and the butter. Add more parsley and basil to the top of each fish and drizzle with the remaining olive oil. Season lightly with sea salt, then wrap the parcels up, tucking the ends under to hold them in position. Bake in the oven for 25 minutes. Serve with boiled new potatoes.

SERVES 4

salmon ceviche with lemon chervil dressing

400 g (14 oz) salmon fillet, skinned
    and deboned
4 tablespoons lemon juice
1 Lebanese (short) cucumber,
    finely diced
2 handfuls of fresh chervil sprigs
4 tablespoons sesame oil

Wrap the salmon fillet in plastic wrap
and put it in the freezer for half an hour.
Remove and slice into paper-thin slices.
Divide the slices among four serving
plates. Spoon the lemon juice over the
salmon. Scatter with the diced cucumber
and the chervil sprigs. At the last minute,
drizzle with the sesame oil and season
lightly with sea salt.

SERVES 4

vegies

full of goodness for all

DUTCH CARROTS WITH HONEY GLAZE
GREEN BEANS WITH TOMATO
SPICED BROCCOLI AND SWEET POTATO
SALT AND PEPPER ZUCCHINI
CAULIFLOWER WITH PEPPERED PARMESAN OIL
TAMARI ROAST PUMPKIN WITH TOFU
CUCUMBER SALAD
BAKED POTATOES WITH GRUYERE AND PROSCIUTTO
CORN WITH SPICED BUTTER
SPICED EGGPLANT AND SPINACH
ROAST NEW POTATOES WITH LEMON AND ROSEMARY

Dutch carrots with honey glaze

20 Dutch carrots, trimmed
   and peeled
1 teaspoon honey
1 tablespoon butter
1 tablespoon sesame seeds

Bring a large pot of salted water to the boil.
Drop the carrots into the water and cook
for 4 minutes, then drain.

Heat the honey and butter in a large
non-stick frying pan over a medium heat,
then add the carrots. Swirl the carrots in
the hot butter, then add the sesame seeds
and cook for 5 minutes, turning the carrots
over every minute or so, until the sesame
seeds are golden.

SERVES 4

left: salt and pepper zucchini
centre: spiced broccoli and sweet potato
right: green beans with tomato

salt and pepper zucchini

2 tablespoons cornflour (cornstarch)
1 teaspoon sea salt
½ teaspoon white pepper
500 g (1 lb 2 oz) zucchini (courgettes)
60 ml (2 fl oz/¼ cup) peanut oil
lemon wedges to serve

Put the cornflour, salt and pepper in a plastic bag. Shake a few times to mix well. Slice the zucchini on the diagonal into long slices approximately 1 cm thick. Put the zucchini pieces in the bag with the cornflour mix and toss until all the zucchini is well coated.

Heat the peanut oil in a large frying pan and pan-fry the zucchini until golden brown on both sides. Drain on paper towel, then arrange on a serving platter with wedges of lemon.

SERVES 4

spiced broccoli and sweet potato

½ teaspoon ground cumin
½ teaspoon ground turmeric
½ teaspoon ground chilli powder
3 tablespoons olive oil
300 g (10½ oz) sweet potato, peeled and cut into 2 cm (¾ in) cubes
500 g (1 lb 2 oz) broccoli florets
100 g (3½ oz) Greek-style yoghurt

Preheat the oven to 200°C (400°F/Gas 6). In a small bowl, combine the spices and the olive oil.

Put the sweet potato in a large bowl and add half the flavoured oil. Toss several times to ensure the sweet potato is well coated in the oil, then put in an ovenproof dish. Cover with foil and bake in the oven for 10 minutes.

Add the broccoli and remaining oil to the bowl and toss to ensure the broccoli is well coated. Remove the foil from the ovenproof dish and shake the sweet potato a few times before adding the broccoli. Bake uncovered for a further 15 minutes.

Put the vegetables on a serving platter and dollop with the yoghurt.

SERVES 4

green beans with tomato

2 tablespoons olive oil
2 large ripe tomatoes, diced
2 garlic cloves, crushed
1 teaspoon sea salt
1 tablespoon soy sauce
125 ml (4½ fl oz/½ cup) water
250 g (9 oz) green beans, trimmed
250 g (9 oz) flat beans, trimmed and
    cut into 3 pieces

Heat the oil in a deep-sided frying pan
and add the tomatoes, garlic, sea salt, soy
sauce and water. Simmer over a medium
heat for 5 minutes or until the tomatoes are
soft, then add the beans. Cover the pan
with a lid and allow to cook for 5 minutes.

Remove from the heat and season with
freshly ground black pepper.

SERVES 4

cauliflower with peppered parmesan oil

45 g (1¾ oz/½ cup) finely grated
    parmesan cheese
2 tablespoons extra virgin olive oil
2 tablespoons light olive oil
500 g (1 lb 2 oz) cauliflower
2 handfuls of flat-leaf (Italian) parsley
    leaves, roughly chopped

In a small bowl, combine the parmesan
and olive oils. Season with sea salt and
freshly ground black pepper.

Bring a pot of salted water to the boil.
Divide the cauliflower into florets, then add
to the boiling water. Cook for 4–5 minutes
or until cooked through, then drain.

Put the cauliflower in a serving bowl and
add the parmesan oil. Toss gently so that
the cauliflower is well coated in the oil.
Add the parsley and serve.

SERVES 4

tamari roast pumpkin with tofu

1 tablespoon tamari
1 tablespoon honey
2 tablespoons olive oil
500 g (1 lb 2 oz) jap pumpkin, cut into 2 cm (¾ in) cubes
50 g (1¾ oz) baby English spinach leaves
100 g (3½ oz) tofu, cut into 1 cm (½ in) cubes
1 spring onion (scallion), finely sliced
1 tablespoon sweet mirin
1 tablespoon sesame seeds

Preheat the oven to 180°C (350°F/Gas 4). Line a baking tray with baking paper.

Put the tamari, honey and 1 tablespoon of the olive oil in a large bowl and stir until combined. Add the pumpkin and toss until it is well coated in the marinade. Pour the pumpkin onto the prepared tray and bake in the oven for 30 minutes or until the pumpkin is cooked through.

Arrange the spinach leaves on a serving plate and top with the cooked pumpkin, tofu and spring onion.

Put the mirin and remaining tablespoon of olive oil in a small bowl, stir to combine, then pour over the salad.

Heat a small pan over a medium heat and add the sesame seeds. Move the seeds over the hot surface until they are beginning to turn golden brown, then spoon them over the salad.

SERVES 4

cucumber salad

3 Lebanese (short) cucumbers
2 small red chillies, seeded and finely
    chopped
1 red capsicum (pepper), finely
    julienned
4 teaspoons sesame oil
1 teaspoon lemon juice

Peel the cucumbers, then slice in half
lengthways. Using the tip of a teaspoon
remove the seeds, then slice the cucumber
on the diagonal. Put the cucumber slices in
a bowl and add the chilli, capsicum,
sesame oil and lemon juice. Toss to
combine and season with a little sea salt.

SERVES 4

baked potatoes with gruyère and prosciutto

4 large floury potatoes
2 tablespoons fine sea salt
200 g (7 oz) light sour cream
100 g (3½ oz/1¾ cup) finely grated gruyère cheese
6 slices prosciutto
1 ripe tomato, finely diced
a handful of baby rocket (arugula) leaves

Preheat the oven to 200°C (400°F/Gas 6).

Wash the potatoes well and while still damp sprinkle with sea salt. Place the potatoes in the oven on a baking tray and bake for an hour or until they are well cooked. When cooked, they will give slightly when pressed with a finger and will have dry, crackly skin.

Combine the sour cream and gruyère in a bowl and season with a little freshly ground black pepper.

Cut the prosciutto slices in half crossways and lightly fry in a non-stick frying pan until crisp and golden. Drain on paper towel.

When the potatoes are cooked break them open, then dollop with the sour cream and cheese mixture, diced tomato and rocket before topping with the crisp prosciutto.

SERVES 4

corn with spiced butter

1 red capsicum (pepper)
2 tablespoons salted butter
¼ teaspoon smoked paprika
a pinch of cayenne pepper
a handful of coriander (cilantro) leaves
4 corn cobs, husks removed

Roast the capsicum on an open fire or under a griller (broiler) until the skin is blackened and blistered all over. Put the capsicum in a bowl and cover with plastic wrap. When cool, remove the skin by rubbing it away from the flesh. Remove the seeds and stem.

Put the capsicum flesh in a blender or food processor and add the butter, paprika, cayenne pepper and coriander leaves. Process, then remove and spoon into a serving bowl.

Bring a large pot of salted water to the boil. Cut the corn cobs into 4–5 cm (1½–2 in) lengths, then add the corn to the boiling water. Cook for 5 minutes, then remove to a large bowl. Add the spiced butter, season with sea salt and freshly ground black pepper and toss until the butter has melted over the corn.

SERVES 4

spiced eggplant and spinach

1 teaspoon finely grated fresh ginger
2 red chillies, seeded and finely chopped
1 garlic clove, minced
1 teaspoon sesame oil
4 tablespoons olive oil
350 g (12 oz) eggplant (aubergine), diced
1 bunch of English spinach, washed and trimmed

Put all the ingredients except the spinach in a bowl and toss together so that the eggplant is completely coated in the oil and flavourings.

Heat a wok over a high heat and add the eggplant. Stir it over the hot surface of the wok until the eggplant is golden on all sides. Add the spinach and toss several times until the spinach is soft and emerald green.

SERVES 4

roast new potatoes with lemon and rosemary

1 kg (2 lb 4 oz) washed new potatoes
60 ml (2 fl oz/¼ cup) olive oil
juice of 1 lemon
6 rosemary sprigs

Preheat the oven to 180°C (350°F/Gas 4).

Put the potatoes in a large pan of cold water and bring to the boil. When the water is boiling, cover the pan with a lid and remove from the heat. Allow to sit for 15 minutes, then drain.

Put the boiled potatoes on a baking tray and with the back of a large spoon lightly crush each potato until it just begins to split. Drizzle the potatoes with the olive oil and lemon juice, then add the rosemary and a generous sprinkle of sea salt. Bake in the oven for 40 minutes or until crisp and golden brown.

SERVES 6

zest

for life with lemon and lime

ZUCCHINI AND CAPER SPAGHETTINI
FIG, APPLE AND GORGONZOLA SALAD
CHINESE PORK WITH ORANGE SALAD   CHICKEN PHO
BAKED FENNEL AND SPINACH PASTA
BAKED ASPARAGUS WITH FETA
AVOCADO WITH FENNEL AND TOMATO SALSA   GAZPACHO
ROAST DUCK WITH A GREEN MANGO SALAD
GREEN CHILLI AND LEMON CHICKEN WITH COUSCOUS
ROAST CHICKEN LEG QUARTERS WITH FIGS AND ALMONDS

zucchini and caper spaghettini

4 tablespoons extra virgin olive oil
2 garlic cloves, crushed
6 medium zucchini (courgettes), grated
300 g (10½ oz) spaghettini
10 oregano leaves, finely chopped
2 tablespoons small salted capers, rinsed
juice of 1 lemon
70 g (2½ oz) grated parmesan cheese

Bring a large saucepan of salted water to the boil.

Heat a deep frying pan over a medium heat and add the olive oil and garlic. Move the garlic around the pan with a spatula until it is lightly golden, then add the grated zucchini. Slowly braise the zucchini, stirring it as it cooks, for about 15 minutes, or until it begins to dry out and catch on the bottom of the pan.

Cook the pasta until it is *al dente*, then drain and return to the warm saucepan. Add the oregano, capers, lemon juice, most of the parmesan and the zucchini. Toss the ingredients together and divide the pasta among four warm pasta bowls. Sprinkle with the remaining parmesan.

SERVES 4

opposite: fig, apple and gorgonzola salad

fig, apple and gorgonzola salad

1 teaspoon lemon juice
2 tablespoons extra virgin olive oil
100 g (3½ oz/2¼ cups) baby rocket
    (arugula) leaves
4 figs, quartered
1 pink lady apple, finely sliced
100 g (3½ oz) gorgonzola cheese

In a small bowl combine the lemon juice
and olive oil and stir to combine. Season
lightly with sea salt and freshly ground
black pepper.

Divide the rocket among four serving
plates. Arrange the fig and apple pieces on
top of the rocket, then crumble the
gorgonzola over the salads. Spoon the
dressing over the top.

SERVES 4

Chinese pork with orange salad

100 g (3½ oz/2¼ cups) baby English
    spinach leaves
400 g (14 oz) Chinese barbecued pork
    (char sui), thinly sliced
2 oranges
2 spring onions (scallions), finely
    sliced
40 g (1½ oz/⅓ cup) unsalted
    pistachios, roughly chopped

Arrange the spinach leaves on a serving
platter and top with the barbecued pork.

With a sharp knife remove the outer skin
and pith from the oranges. Remove the
orange segments by running the blade of
the knife between the individual
membranes, and arrange the segments on
top of the pork. Do this over the salad so
that the juice runs onto the pork. Top with
the spring onions and pistachios.

SERVES 4

chicken pho

225 g (8 oz) dried rice sticks
1.5 litres (52 fl oz/6 cups) good quality chicken stock
2 free-range chicken breasts, thinly sliced against the grain
10 g (¼ oz/½ cup) mint leaves
15 g (½ oz/½ cup) coriander (cilantro) leaves
20 g (¾ oz/½ cup) holy basil leaves
100 g (3½ oz) mung bean sprouts
2 red chillies, seeded and finely sliced
80 g (2¾ oz/½ cup) fried shallots
1 lime, quartered
fish sauce

Place the rice sticks in a large bowl and cover with warm water. Allow them to soak for half an hour or until they are soft.

Place the chicken stock in a saucepan over a medium heat and bring to a soft rolling boil. Reduce the heat.

Fill another large saucepan with water and bring it to the boil. Divide the noodles into four batches and cook each batch separately, lowering it into the boiling water with a sieve. Each batch of noodles will need only about 10 seconds. Put the noodles in four bowls, then put the chicken in the sieve and blanch for about 2 minutes. Put the chicken in the four bowls and top with the chicken stock. Garnish with the herbs, mung bean sprouts, chilli and fried shallots. Serve with the lime and fish sauce as extra seasoning.

SERVES 4

baked fennel and spinach pasta

2 fennel bulbs, trimmed and diced
3 tablespoons olive oil
300 g (10½ oz) casarecci pasta
2 tablespoons lemon juice
100 g (3½ oz) baby English spinach
    leaves
70 g (2½ oz/¾ cup) finely grated
    parmesan cheese

Preheat the oven to 180°C (350°F/Gas 4).
Bring a large pot of salted water to the boil.

Line a baking tray with baking paper and
add the fennel and olive oil. Toss to ensure
all the fennel is well coated in the olive oil,
then season with sea salt and freshly
ground black pepper. Bake in the oven for
15 minutes or until the fennel is soft and
beginning to darken on the edges. Remove.

Cook the casarecci until *al dente*. Drain
and return to the warm saucepan. Add the
fennel and juices from the baking tray,
lemon juice and spinach leaves. Toss
several times then divide among four pasta
bowls. Top with the parmesan and a few
sprigs of fennel fronds.

SERVES 4

baked asparagus with feta

32 asparagus spears
2 tablespoons olive oil
10 mint leaves
a handful of flat-leaf (Italian) parsley
    leaves
1 tablespoon lemon juice
1 teaspoon finely chopped preserved
    lemon rind
50 g (1¾ oz) Bulgarian feta cheese

Preheat the oven to 200°C (400°F/Gas 6).

Trim the asparagus of any woody stems,
brush with the oil and season with freshly
ground black pepper. Place the stems in a
single layer on a baking tray and roast,
turning occasionally for about 10 minutes,
or until tender and slightly darkened.
Season with sea salt. Arrange on a serving
platter with the mint and parsley leaves.

Combine the lemon juice and preserved
lemon and spoon over the asparagus. To
finish, crumble the feta over the top.

SERVES 4

opposite: avocado with
fennel and tomato salsa
this page: gazpacho

avocado with fennel and tomato salsa

a handful of coriander (cilantro) leaves
1 red chilli, seeded and finely chopped
1 small ripe tomato, finely diced
4 marinated artichoke hearts, finely sliced
2 tablespoons extra virgin olive oil
1 teaspoon balsamic vinegar
2 ripe avocados
1 large fennel bulb, finely sliced

Put the coriander leaves, chilli, tomato and artichoke hearts in a small bowl and add the olive oil and vinegar. Season lightly with sea salt and freshly ground black pepper. Toss lightly to combine.

Cut the avocados in half and remove the stones. Run a large serving spoon between the flesh and skin and remove the avocado flesh in one smooth movement. Cut each avocado half into three thick slices. Arrange the sliced avocado halves on serving plates with the fennel, then top with the tomato salsa.

SERVES 4

gazpacho

1 red capsicum (pepper)
750 g (1 lb 10 oz) ripe tomatoes, chopped
150 g (5½ oz) cucumbers, chopped
1 tablespoon sea salt
1 garlic clove, roughly chopped
50 g (1¾ oz) sourdough bread, crusts trimmed
80 ml (2½ fl oz/⅓ cup) dry sherry
125 ml (4½ fl oz/½ cup) water
Tabasco sauce
celery stalks or basil leaves for serving

Roast the capsicum on an open fire or under a griller (broiler) until the skin is blackened and blistered all over. Put the capsicum in a bowl and cover with plastic wrap. When cool remove the skin by rubbing it away from the flesh. Remove the seeds and stem.

Put the tomatoes and cucumber in a bowl and sprinkle with the sea salt. Stir a few times, then set aside for 15 minutes.

Add the garlic, sourdough and capsicum to the tomatoes and cucumber, then process in a blender or food processor until smooth. Pour into a serving bowl or large jug and add the sherry and the water. Stir to combine, then add Tabasco a drop at a time until it suits your taste. Season to taste with sea salt. Chill in the fridge until ready to serve. Serve with celery stalks or finely chopped basil leaves.

SERVES 4

roast duck with a green mango salad

1 Chinese roast duck
2 green mangoes, julienned or grated
3 tablespoons plum sauce
4 tablespoons lime juice
1 teaspoon sesame oil
1 red large red chilli, seeded and chopped
a handful of coriander (cilantro) leaves
150 g (5½ oz/3⅓ cups) baby rocket (arugula) leaves

Remove the skin from the roast duck and cut it into thin strips with a pair of kitchen scissors. Lay the skin strips on a tray and set to one side. Remove the meat from the roast duck and shred it into thin strips.

Put the mango in a bowl and add the plum sauce, lime juice and sesame oil. Stir to combine, then add the chilli and coriander.

Arrange the rocket on a serving platter, then top with the shredded duck meat. Cover with the dressed green mango.

Grill the duck skin until crisp, then drain on paper towel. Arrange the crisp skin on top of the mango and serve.

SERVES 4

green chilli and lemon chicken with couscous

4 small chicken breast fillets
juice of 1 lemon
100 ml (3½ fl oz) olive oil
2 garlic cloves, crushed
185 g (6½ oz/1 cup) couscous
1 teaspoon ground cumin
1 tablespoon butter
250 ml (9 fl oz/1 cup) boiling water
250 g (9 oz) cherry tomatoes, quartered
1 Lebanese (short) cucumber, diced
10 mint leaves
1 large green chilli, seeded and finely chopped
a handful of coriander (cilantro) leaves
2 spring onions (scallions), finely sliced

Preheat the oven to 180°C (350°F/Gas 4).

Cut the chicken breasts into thin strips. Put the chicken strips in a large ceramic ovenproof dish. Whisk together the lemon juice, olive oil and garlic, then pour the mixture over the chicken strips. Marinate for at least 10 minutes.

Bake the chicken in the oven for 20 minutes.

Put the couscous, cumin and butter in a small bowl and pour the boiling water over it. Cover the bowl with plastic wrap and allow the couscous mix to soak for 10 minutes. Fluff with a fork, season with freshly ground black pepper and divide among four bowls.

Put the chicken strips and cooking liquid in a bowl and season with sea salt. Allow to cool a little then add the tomatoes, cucumber, mint, chilli, coriander and spring onion. Toss a few times then spoon over the couscous.

SERVES 4

la fourchet

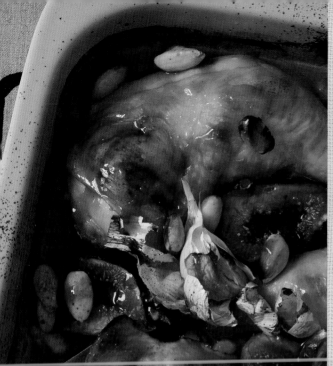

roast chicken leg quarters with figs and almonds

4 chicken leg quarters
4 figs, halved
80 g (2¾ oz/½ cup) blanched almonds
4 garlic cloves, crushed
juice of 2 lemons
2 tablespoons honey
green salad to serve

Preheat the oven to 180°C (350°F/Gas 4).

Put the chicken, figs, almonds and garlic into a roasting tin. Pour over the lemon juice, then drizzle with the honey. Season with sea salt, then cover the roasting tin with foil. Bake for 40 minutes, then remove the foil and bake for a further 20 minutes.

Serve with a green salad.

SERVES 4

bite

into the seasoned and savoury

DUCK BREAST WITH CELERY, APPLES AND PECANS
LAMB CUTLETS WITH CHUNKY TABOULEH
PORK CUTLETS WITH LEMON THYME MARINADE
POLENTA-CRUSTED CHICKEN WITH WATERCRESS AND TOMATO SALAD
ROAST BEEF AND THAI BASIL SALAD
LAMB FILLET WITH GREEN PEA CURRY
BARBECUED CHICKEN WITH CUCUMBER AND MANGO SALSA
PORK RIBS WITH BLACK BEANS AND CORN
MINUTE STEAK WITH EGGPLANT, CAPSICUM AND CHICKPEAS
LAMB CUTLETS WITH CARROTS
SAUSAGES WITH FRESH TOMATO SAUCE
VEAL CUTLETS WITH WHITE BEANS

duck breast with celery, apples and pecans

2 tablespoons dark brown sugar
2 teaspoons sea salt
4 boneless duck breasts, skin on
200 g (7 oz) celery, finely sliced
2 red apples, cored and finely sliced
100 g (3½ oz) pecans, roughly chopped
a handful of flat-leaf (Italian) parsley leaves
3 tablespoons lemon juice
2 tablespoons maple syrup

Preheat the oven to 200°C (400°F/Gas 6).

In a small bowl combine the sugar and salt. Using a sharp knife, lightly score the skin of the duck breasts in a crisscross pattern, then rub the sugar and salt mixture into the duck skin.

Put the duck breasts on a rack set over a baking tray and roast in the oven for 12 minutes, then place under a hot grill (broiler) for 4 minutes or until the skin is crisp and golden brown. Remove the tray from under the grill, cover with foil and allow the duck to rest for a few minutes.

Combine the celery, apple, pecans, parsley, lemon juice and maple syrup in a bowl and toss to combine. Arrange the salad on four plates.

Slice the duck breast diagonally across the grain and arrange the slices over the salad.

SERVES 4

lamb cutlets with chunky tabouleh

50 g (1¾ oz/¼ cup) burghul (bulgur)
1 teaspoon ground cumin
2 tomatoes, diced
a handful of parsley, roughly chopped
10 mint leaves, finely sliced
1 spring onion (scallion), finely sliced
2 tablespoons olive oil
1 tablespoon lemon juice
12 lamb cutlets, French trimmed

Put the burghul in a small bowl with the cumin and cover with cold water. Soak
for 10 minutes, then drain and squeeze to remove any excess liquid. Put it in a large bowl
along with the tomatoes, parsley, mint, spring onion, olive oil and lemon juice. Season lightly
with sea salt and freshly ground black pepper, then toss to combine.

Barbecue or grill (broil) the cutlets for 2–3 minutes on each side. Place them on a warm
plate, season with sea salt and cover with foil for a few minutes to rest.

Divide the chunky tabouleh among four plates, then top with the cutlets and drizzle with
any meat juices.

SERVES 4

opposite: duck breast with celery, apples and pecans
this page: lamb cutlets with chunky tabouleh

pork cutlets with lemon thyme marinade

1 teaspoon fennel seeds
1 tablespoon lemon thyme leaves
juice of 1 lemon
4 x 150 g (5½ oz) pork cutlets
2 fennel bulbs
2 tablespoons finely chopped flat-leaf (Italian) parsley
2 tablespoons extra virgin olive oil
3 tablespoons butter
2 tablespoons dry sherry or white wine

Grind the fennel seeds with a mortar and pestle until roughly broken up. Add the ground fennel seeds to a bowl with the thyme, lemon juice and pork cutlets. Toss several times to ensure that the cutlets are well coated in the marinade.

Finely slice the fennel and put it in a bowl with the parsley and olive oil. Season lightly with sea salt and freshly ground black pepper. Toss to combine, then set aside.

Heat 1 tablespoon of the butter in a large frying pan over a medium heat until it has melted and begins to bubble. Add the pork cutlets, reserving the remaining marinade, and cook for 3 minutes. Turn the cutlets over and reduce the heat to low, then cook for a further 4 minutes. Transfer the cutlets to a warm plate, season lightly with sea salt, cover with foil and set aside.

Return the pan to the heat and add the reserved marinade and sherry or wine. Stir with a wooden spoon to lift any of the pan juices from the base of the pan, then add the remaining butter. Stir to combine, then remove from the heat.

Divide the fennel among four plates, then add the cutlets and a spoonful of butter sauce.

SERVES 4

polenta-crusted chicken with watercress and tomato salad

150 g (5½ oz/1 cup) fine polenta
1 teaspoon ground cumin
1 teaspoon paprika
2 teaspoons dried oregano
3 chicken breasts
4 tablespoons light olive oil plus extra for frying
2 large ripe tomatoes
2 tablespoons extra virgin olive oil
1 tablespoon balsamic vinegar
2 handfuls of picked watercress sprigs

Put the polenta, cumin, paprika and oregano in a bowl.

Slice the chicken breasts lengthways into 1 cm (½ in) thick slices and put in a bowl with the light olive oil. Toss to ensure that all the slices are coated in the oil.

One at a time, dip the chicken pieces in the polenta and toss so that they are completely coated. Place on a clean tray.

Heat a non-stick frying pan over a medium to high heat and add a tablespoon of light olive oil. Fry the chicken pieces until golden brown on all sides, adding extra olive oil when necessary. Drain on paper towel.

Finely dice the tomatoes and put them in a bowl with the extra virgin olive oil and the vinegar. Season with sea salt and freshly ground black pepper.

Divide the watercress among four serving plates and spoon the tomato salad onto it. Top with the cooked chicken pieces and drizzle with any remaining dressing.

SERVES 4

roast beef and Thai basil salad

400 g (14 oz) beef fillet
1 tablespoon vegetable oil
2 tablespoons lemon juice
1 tablespoon light olive oil
1 tablespoon soy sauce
1 tablespoon finely grated fresh ginger
1 teaspoon wasabi paste
1 teaspoon sesame oil
1 garlic clove, crushed
½ teaspoon wholegrain mustard
2 spring onions (scallions), finely sliced
250 g (9 oz) cherry tomatoes, halved
1 Lebanese (short) cucumber, thinly sliced on the diagonal
2 large red chillies, seeded and finely sliced
1 bunch Thai basil, leaves removed
2 ripe avocados, flesh diced

Preheat the oven to 220°C (425°F/Gas 7).

Trim the beef of all fat and sinew. Heat a frying pan or chargrill pan over a high heat. When the pan is hot add the vegetable oil then sear the beef on all sides. Transfer to a baking tray and cook in the oven for 12 minutes. Remove to a plate. Season with sea salt and cover with foil. Allow to rest until it has cooled.

Stir together the lemon juice, olive oil, soy sauce, ginger, wasabi paste, sesame oil, garlic and mustard in a small bowl.

Finely slice the beef and put it in a bowl. Add the meat juices then pour the dressing over the beef. Add the spring onion, cherry tomatoes, cucumber, chilli and Thai basil leaves. Toss lightly to combine then divide among four serving plates. Top with the diced avocado and drizzle with any remaining dressing.

SERVES 4

lamb fillet with green pea curry

4 tablespoons light olive oil
4 teaspoons brown mustard seeds
2 teaspoons grated fresh ginger
2 large white onions, thinly sliced
2 teaspoons ground cumin
2 teaspoons ground turmeric
2 red chillies, seeded and finely chopped
4 large ripe tomatoes, cut into chunks
250 ml (9 fl oz/1 cup) water
500 g (1 lb 2 oz/3¼ cup) frozen green peas
2 tablespoons finely chopped mint
500 g (1 lb 2 oz) lamb backstrap
extra mint leaves to serve

Preheat the oven to 220°C (425°F/Gas 7).

Heat the olive oil in a deep frying pan and put in the mustard seeds. As the seeds begin
to pop, add the ginger, onion and a little sea salt and cook until the onion is soft. Mix in the
cumin, turmeric and chilli and cook for a minute, then add the tomatoes and the water.
Simmer for 2 minutes, then add the peas and mint. Cover and cook for 15 minutes or until
the peas are tender. Season to taste with sea salt and freshly ground black pepper.

Heat a non-stick frying pan over a medium to high heat, then sear the lamb backstrap on
both sides until well browned. Transfer to a baking tray and cook in the oven for 5 minutes.
Remove and cover with foil for a few minutes.

Spoon the curry into the centre of four serving plates. Slice the lamb against the grain into
thin slices and arrange over the top of the curry. Drizzle with some of the meat juices and
sprinkle with a few whole mint leaves.

SERVES 4

opposite: roast beef and Thai basil salad
this page: lamb fillet with green pea curry

barbecued chicken with cucumber and mango salsa

4 chicken leg quarters
1 mango, just ripe
1 Lebanese (short) cucumber, finely diced
2 spring onions (scallions), finely sliced
1 red chilli, seeded and finely chopped
1 bunch coriander (cilantro), leaves only
juice of 2 limes

Heat a barbecue or grill plate and cook the chicken pieces skin side down for 10 minutes over a medium heat. Turn the chicken pieces over, cover with foil and cook for a further 10 minutes. Remove to a warm plate, season with sea salt and freshly ground black pepper, cover with foil again and leave to rest.

Remove the flesh from the mango and finely dice it. Put the diced mango flesh in a bowl with the cucumber, spring onion, chilli, coriander leaves and lime juice. Toss to combine.

Put the chicken pieces onto serving plates and spoon the salsa over them.

SERVES 4

pork ribs with black beans and corn

2 tablespoons tomato paste (concentrated purée)
2 tablespoons honey
2 tablespoons soy sauce
2 teaspoons sesame oil
2 teaspoons finely grated orange zest
4 thick pork ribs, approximately 600 g (1 lb 5 oz)
2 tablespoons olive oil
1 red onion, finely diced
1 teaspoon smoked paprika
2 corn cobs, kernels removed
400 g (14 oz) tinned black beans, drained and rinsed
a handful of coriander (cilantro) leaves

Preheat the oven to 180°C (350°F/Gas 4).

Combine the tomato paste, honey, soy sauce, sesame oil and orange zest in a bowl. Add the pork ribs and toss so that they are well coated in the marinade. Put onto a baking tray and bake in the oven for 30 minutes, turning once.

Meanwhile put the olive oil in a deep-sided frying pan and add the onion and paprika. Cook over a medium heat until the onion is soft, then add the corn kernels. Cook the corn until it has turned a golden yellow then add the black beans and lightly stir to combine. Season with sea salt and freshly ground black pepper.

Divide the corn and black beans among four warm plates, then add the pork ribs. Top with the coriander leaves.

SERVES 4

minute steak with eggplant, capsicum and chickpeas

400 g (14 oz) sirloin steak
2 tablespoons olive oil
170 g (6 oz) eggplant (aubergine), diced
1 garlic clove, minced
1 red capsicum (pepper), diced
400 g (14 oz) tinned chickpeas, drained
12 basil leaves

Trim the piece of steak of all fat and sinew. Then slice into four thinner steaks.

Heat the olive oil in a deep-sided pan over a medium heat and add the eggplant. Cook the eggplant, stirring occasionally until it is golden brown then add the garlic and capsicum. Cook for a further 2 minutes. Remove from the heat and add the chickpeas and basil leaves. Toss to combine.

Cook the steaks on a barbecue or grill plate for a minute on each side. Put the steaks on to four warm plates, then spoon the vegetables over the steaks.

SERVES 4

lamb cutlets with carrots

500 g (1 lb 2 oz) carrots
1 tablespoon butter
1 tablespoon pomegranate molasses
a handful of flat-leaf (Italian) parsley leaves
12 lamb cutlets, French trimmed
green salad to serve

Bring a pot of salted water to the boil. Peel the carrots, then cut them into
2 cm (¾ in) discs. Add them to the boiling water and cook for 15–20 minutes.

Put the butter, pomegranate molasses and parsley in a bowl.

Barbecue or grill (broil) the cutlets for 2–3 minutes on each side. Place them on a warm
plate, season with sea salt and cover with foil for a few minutes to rest.

Drain the cooked carrots and add them to the bowl. Toss to ensure that the carrots are well
coated in the molasses. Season them lightly with sea salt and freshly ground black pepper.
Serve with the cutlets and a green salad.

SERVES 4

sausages with fresh tomato sauce

2 tablespoons olive oil
1 red onion, finely sliced
500 g (1 lb 2 oz) ripe tomatoes, chopped
1 tablespoon tomato paste (concentrated purée)
1 scant tablespoon sea salt
8 good quality beef sausages
15 fresh oregano leaves

Heat the olive oil in a saucepan over a medium heat and add the onion. Sauté until the onion is soft, then add the tomato, tomato paste and sea salt. Reduce the heat to low, cover the saucepan with a lid and allow to simmer for half an hour.

Meanwhile, grill (broil) the sausages until they are cooked through. Divide the sausages among four warm plates. Add the fresh oregano leaves to the sauce, then spoon the sauce over the sausages.

Serve with steamed greens and mashed potato or couscous.

SERVES 4

veal cutlets with white beans

400 g (14 oz) tinned white beans,
    rinsed and drained
12 green olives, sliced
6 basil leaves, shredded
12 cherry tomatoes, halved
4 veal cutlets
2 tablespoons extra virgin olive oil
lemon wedges and green salad to serve

Preheat the oven to 180°C (350°F/Gas 4).

In a bowl, combine the white beans, olives, basil and tomatoes. Season with sea salt and freshly ground black pepper.

Heat a large non-stick frying pan over a high heat. Add the veal cutlets and sear for 2 minutes, then turn and sear for 1 minute. Place the cutlets on a baking tray and bake for 8 minutes. Remove from the oven, then cover loosely with foil and allow to rest for 5 minutes.

Divide the white bean salad among four plates, then top with the veal cutlets. Drizzle with the olive oil and serve with a lemon wedge and green salad.

SERVES 4

slice

and share the good times

GOATS CHEESE TOASTIE   STRACCHINO AND SALAMI PIZZA
ZUCCHINI, TOMATO AND PESTO PIZZA
HAM AND MUSHROOM CALZONE   STEAK SANDWICH
PUMPKIN AND CHILLI QUESADILLAS
BURGER WITH BEETROOT SLICES   SALMON AND PASTRY BAKE
WHITE CHOCOLATE AND RASPBERRY SLICE
CHOCOLATE CRUNCH WITH FRESH RASPBERRIES

goats cheese toastie

4 slices rye bread, crusts removed
150 g (5½ oz) goats cheese, sliced
125 g (4½ oz) cherry tomatoes, halved
1 yellow capsicum (pepper), finely
    diced
100 g (3½ oz) marinated artichoke
    hearts, drained and quartered
10 basil leaves
a handful of flat-leaf (Italian) parsley
    leaves
2 tablespoons extra virgin olive oil
1 teaspoon balsamic vinegar

Preheat the oven to 200°C (400°F/Gas 6).

Put the bread slices on a baking tray and
arrange the goats cheese over the top.
Bake in the oven until the goats cheese is
golden brown on top.

Meanwhile, put the remaining ingredients
in a bowl. Season with sea salt and freshly
ground black pepper and toss to combine.

Arrange the bread slices on four plates and
top with the tomato salad.

SERVES 4

stracchino and salami pizza

140 g (5 oz) tomato paste (concentrated purée)
1 teaspoon dried oregano
2 x 23 cm (9 in) pizza bases (see Store, page 241)
12 slices salami
300 g (10½ oz) stracchino cheese (see Glossary, page 249), thinly sliced
2 tablespoons grated parmesan cheese
30 fresh oregano leaves

Preheat the oven to 220°C (425°F/Gas 7).

Put the tomato paste in a small saucepan with the oregano and cook it over a medium heat for a few minutes, stirring continuously. Remove from the heat.

Spread the tomato paste over the two pizza bases. Arrange the salami and cheese over the top of the pizza and sprinkle with the parmesan. Bake for 10 minutes or until the pizza base is golden and crispy. Scatter with the fresh oregano leaves.

SERVES 4

zucchini, tomato and pesto pizza

140 g (5 oz) tomato paste (concentrated purée)
1 teaspoon dried oregano
4 tablespoons pesto sauce (see Store, page 242)
2 x 23 cm (9 in) pizza bases (see Store, page 241)
2 zucchini (courgettes) (approximately 250 g/9 oz)
250 g (9 oz) cherry tomatoes, quartered
100 g (3½ oz) mozzarella cheese, grated
4 tablespoons grated parmesan cheese
fresh basil leaves to serve

Preheat the oven to 220°C (425°F/Gas 7).
Put the tomato paste in a small saucepan with the
oregano and cook it over a medium heat for a few
minutes, stirring continuously. Remove from the
heat and stir the pesto through the tomato paste.

Spread the sauce over the pizza bases.

Using a vegetable peeler, thinly slice the zucchini into
ribbons and pile them on top of the pizzas. Arrange the
tomato quarters over the zucchini, then top with the
mozzarella and parmesan.

Bake in the oven for 10 minutes or until the pizza base
is golden and crisp. Scatter with fresh basil leaves.

SERVES 4

ham and mushroom calzone

140 g (5 oz) tomato paste
   (concentrated purée)
1 teaspoon dried oregano
2 x 23 cm (9 in) pizza bases
   (see Store, page 241)
80 g (2¾ oz) leg ham, thinly sliced
60 g (2¼ oz/⅔ cup) button
   mushrooms, finely sliced
60 g (2¼ oz) mozzarella cheese,
   grated
100 g (3½ oz) ricotta cheese
10 kalamata olives, pitted and
   finely chopped
10 leaves basil

Preheat the oven to 220°C (425°F/Gas 7).

Put the tomato paste in a small saucepan with the oregano and cook it over a medium heat for a few minutes, stirring continuously. Remove from the heat.

Spread each of the pizza bases with the tomato paste, then divide the remaining ingredients between the two pizzas, forming a line of ingredients down the centre. Roll one side of the circle over to form a half moon and press the edges of the pastry together. Gently lift onto an oiled baking tray and bake in the oven for 15 minutes. Serve with a green salad.

SERVES 4

steak sandwich

400 g (14 oz) sirloin steak
1 tablespoon olive oil
6 thyme sprigs
1 large red onion, finely sliced
2 tomatoes, finely sliced
2 tablespoons extra virgin olive oil
8 tablespoons pesto sauce (see Store, page 242)
8 slices fresh sourdough bread
a handful of baby rocket (arugula) leaves

Preheat the oven to 200°C (400°F/Gas 6).

Trim all the fat and sinew from the steak, then with a sharp knife cut it into very thin slices. Put the sliced meat in a bowl and add the olive oil and thyme sprigs. Toss so that the meat is well coated in the oil. Cover with plastic wrap and set to one side.

Line a baking tray with baking paper. Put the onion on one side of the baking tray, then put the tomatoes on the other. Drizzle with the extra virgin olive oil and season lightly with sea salt and freshly ground black pepper. Bake for 20 minutes.

Spread the pesto over the bread. Heat a non-stick frying pan over a high heat and cook the meat slices for 1 minute on each side. As the meat is cooked, pile it onto four of the bread slices. Remove the tomatoes and onion from the oven and add to the sandwiches along with the baby rocket leaves. Top with the remaining bread slices.

SERVES 4

pumpkin and chilli quesadillas

4 tablespoons pitted and chopped black olives
1 large red chilli, seeded and finely chopped
125 ml (4 fl oz/½ cup) light olive oil
500 g (1 lb 2 oz) pumpkin (winter squash)
1 teaspoon smoky paprika
300 g (10½ oz/2 cups) grated mozzarella cheese
150 g (5½ oz/1 cup) crumbled feta cheese
8 x 16 cm (6¼ in) white corn tortillas
2 handfuls of coriander (cilantro) leaves

Preheat the oven to 180°C (350°F/Gas 4).

Put the olives, chilli and olive oil in a blender and blend to create a flavoured oil.

Dice the pumpkin into small pieces and put onto a baking tray. Brush with a little of the chilli oil and sprinkle with the paprika. Bake for 30 minutes or until golden brown and soft.

Put the cheeses in a bowl and toss to combine.

Put one tortilla onto a clean board. Sprinkle with a liberal coating of the mixed cheeses, some of the roast pumpkin and a scattering of coriander leaves. Cover with a second tortilla, brush well with the flavoured oil and set to one side. Repeat with the remaining ingredients. Put the quesadillas onto an oiled baking tray and bake for 7 minutes. Turn the quesadillas over and cook for a further 7 minutes. Remove from the oven and slice into quarters. Serve immediately.

MAKES 16 PIECES

burger with beetroot slices

4 medium beetroot (beets)
1 tablespoon balsamic vinegar
1 tablespoon brown sugar
6 mint leaves, finely sliced
1 large red chilli, seeded and finely chopped
500 g (1 lb 2 oz) minced (ground) pork and veal
1 teaspoon finely grated fresh ginger
1 tablespoon finely chopped lemongrass
½ onion, finely diced
1 tablespoon soy sauce
2 tablespoons tomato paste (concentrated purée)
½ trimmed iceberg lettuce, finely sliced
4 soft burger rolls, split open
a handful of coriander (cilantro) leaves

Put the beetroot in a saucepan and cover with cold water. Bring to the boil and cook for 30 minutes or until the beetroot is cooked through. Drain and allow to cool. Wearing rubber gloves, rub the skins from the beetroot, then thinly slice them into a bowl.

In a small bowl, mix together the vinegar, brown sugar, mint and chilli, stirring until the sugar has dissolved. Pour the dressing over the beetroot and set to one side.

Put the mince, ginger, lemongrass, onion, soy sauce and tomato paste in a large bowl. Season with sea salt and freshly ground black pepper. Knead the ingredients together with your hands then form it into four large patties. Heat a barbecue grill or large non-stick frying pan over a high heat and sear the patties. With a spatula press down to flatten them, before reducing the heat to medium and cooking for 5 minutes. Flip the patties over and continue to cook until the meat is cooked through.

Put the shredded iceberg lettuce onto the open burger rolls and top with the burger, beetroot slices and coriander leaves.

SERVES 4

salmon and pastry bake

1 knob fresh ginger, peeled and roughly chopped
finely grated zest of 1 lemon
4 cm (1½ in) fresh lemongrass, roughly chopped
1 red chilli, seeded and roughly chopped
2 tablespoons brown sugar
1 sheet frozen shortcrust (pie) pastry
2 x 200 g (7 oz) salmon fillets, approximately 5 cm (2 in) wide, skinned and
    deboned
1 tablespoon milk
2 tablespoons sesame seeds
Asian leaf salad to serve

Preheat the oven to 200°C (400°F/Gas 6).

Put the ginger, grated lemon zest, lemongrass, chilli and brown sugar in a mortar and and
work to a rough paste with a pestle.

Put the sheet of pastry on a baking tray lined with baking paper. Lay the two salmon
fillets across the centre of the pastry. Turn one of the salmon pieces upside down and
overlap the two thin ends. This will ensure an evenly shaped rectangle. Top with the
ginger and lemongrass paste. Bring the two sides of the pastry together and roll them
over to join together. Press together, then press the two open ends together. Brush the
milk over the pastry, then sprinkle with the sesame seeds and some sea salt. Bake in the
oven for 30 minutes.

Slice, and serve with the Asian leaf salad.

SERVES 4

white chocolate and raspberry slice

125 g (4½ oz) butter
150 g (5½ oz) white chocolate
175 g (6 oz/¾ cup) caster (superfine) sugar
125 g (4½ oz/1 cup) self-raising flour
90 g (3¼ oz/1 cup) desiccated coconut
2 eggs, beaten
150 g (5½ oz/1¼ cups) fresh raspberries

Preheat the oven to 180°C (350°F/Gas 4).

Grease and line a 16 x 26 cm (6¼ x 10½ in) baking tin.

Melt the butter and white chocolate in a saucepan over a low heat. Add the caster sugar and stir to combine.

Pour into a large bowl and add the flour and coconut. Stir to combine, then add the beaten eggs. Stir lightly to just combine, then fold in the fresh raspberries.

Pour the mixture into the tin and bake for 40 minutes, or until firm. Cool in the tin. Cut into squares and dust with icing sugar.

MAKES 20 PIECES

chocolate crunch with fresh raspberries

250 g (9 oz) dark chocolate
50 g (1¾ oz) butter
3 tablespoons golden syrup
250 g (9 oz) digestive biscuits (cookies)
1 tablespoon cocoa powder
100 g (3½ oz) hazelnut meal
2 tablespoons brandy
fresh raspberries to serve

Line a 15 cm (6 in) square tin or container with baking paper.

Put the chocolate, butter and golden syrup in a small saucepan and melt over a low heat.

In a large bowl crush the digestive biscuits into small pieces, then add the cocoa and hazelnut meal. Pour the melted chocolate over the dry ingredients and stir to combine. Add the brandy and stir a few more times before spooning into the tin. Top with another layer of baking paper and firmly press down to form a smooth top. Refrigerate for several hours.

Slice into small squares and serve with fresh raspberries.

MAKES 25 PIECES

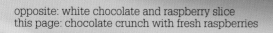
opposite: white chocolate and raspberry slice
this page: chocolate crunch with fresh raspberries

tangy

treats from the tree

ROSE JELLY WITH RASPBERRIES
BLACKBERRY FOOL   PINEAPPLE WITH SWEET SYRUP
APPLE AND VANILLA ICE WITH GRAPEFRUIT
MANGO AND PINEAPPLE JELLIES
NECTARINES WITH YOGHURT, HONEY AND ORANGE FLOWER WATER
STRAWBERRY AND TURKISH DELIGHT SUNDAES
GINGER-SPICED ORANGES WITH CARAMEL ICE CREAM
FRUIT SALAD
POACHED PEACHES WITH FRESH RASPBERRY SORBET

rose jelly with raspberries

400 ml (14 fl oz) rosé wine
2 teaspoons rosewater
150 g (5½ oz/1¾ cup) caster (superfine) sugar
200 ml (7 fl oz) water
1½ tablespoons gelatine powder (see Glossary, page 245)
raspberries and pouring (whipping) cream to serve

Put the rosé, rosewater and sugar in a small saucepan with the water and heat over a medium heat, stirring until the sugar dissolves. Pour 200 ml (7 fl oz) of the warm liquid into a small bowl and add the gelatine. Stir to dissolve, then return the liquid to the remaining sweetened rosé and stir through. Pour into a bowl, cover with plastic wrap and refrigerate for several hours or overnight.

Spoon the jelly into glasses with the fresh raspberries and serve with a jug of pouring cream.

SERVES 4–6

blackberry fool

300 g (10½ oz) frozen blackberries, thawed and drained
3 tablespoons caster (superfine) sugar
2 tablespoons crème de framboise (optional)
1 teaspoon orange flower water
300 ml (10½ fl oz) cream, whipped

Put the blackberries, sugar, liqueur (if using) and orange flower water in a blender or food processor and whiz to a purée (if you don't like seeds, sieve the purée at this point).

Fold the puréed berries into the cream and spoon the mixture into four chilled glasses.

Serve with almond bread or biscotti.

SERVES 6

pineapple with sweet syrup

250 ml (9 fl oz/1 cup) cloudy
    apple juice
200 g (7 oz) brown sugar
3 cardamom pods, split
1 star anise
1 ripe pineapple
1 teaspoon finely grated lime zest
vanilla ice cream to serve

Put the apple juice, brown sugar,
cardamom and star anise in a saucepan
and bring to the boil. Reduce the heat and
allow to simmer for 10 minutes. Remove
from the heat and remove the spices.

Remove the skin and eyes of the pineapple,
then cut into quarters and remove the
tough core. Thinly slice, then place in a
serving bowl.

Just before serving add the lime zest to the
spiced sauce, then pour over the pineapple.
Serve with vanilla ice cream.

SERVES 4–6

apple and vanilla ice with grapefruit

80 g (2¾ oz/⅓ cup) sugar
170 ml (5½ fl oz/⅔ cup) water
1 vanilla bean
1 green apple
200 ml (7 fl oz) cloudy apple juice
2 ruby grapefruit

Put the sugar and water in a saucepan and bring to the boil. Cut the vanilla bean in half lengthways and using a knife scrape the soft beans from the centre. Add them to the saucepan along with the vanilla pod. Stir until the sugar has dissolved, then lower the heat and grate the apple, adding it to the sugar syrup. Remove from the heat and allow to cool. Discard the vanilla pod and add the apple juice, stir, then put the mixture in a plastic container. Place in the freezer for 1 hour. Remove and give the mixture a stir with a fork to break up the crystals. Return to the freezer for another 1–2 hours. Before serving, stir again with a fork to break up the icy texture.

Serve with ruby grapefruit segments.

SERVES 4

mango and pineapple jellies

1 mango
1 tablespoon lemon juice
375 ml (13 fl oz/1½ cups) pineapple juice
110 g (3¾ oz/½ cup) caster (superfine) sugar
1½ tablespoons gelatine powder (see Glossary, page 245)
vanilla ice cream, to serve

Purée the flesh of the mango with the lemon juice. Pour it into a measuring jug.

Put half the pineapple juice and the sugar in a small saucepan over a medium heat. Stir until the sugar has dissolved. Remove from the heat and stir in the gelatine powder. Add to the mango and stir well. Add enough of the remaining pineapple juice to make 600 ml (21 fl oz) of liquid. Pour into four moulds, cover with plastic wrap and refrigerate overnight.

To remove the jellies from the moulds, dip the base of the moulds briefly in warm water, then turn out onto a plate. Serve with vanilla ice cream.

SERVES 4

nectarines with yoghurt, honey and orange flower water

200 g (7 oz) Greek-style yoghurt
1 teaspoon honey
¼ teaspoon orange flower water
6 nectarines, halved
2 tablespoons brown sugar

Combine the yoghurt, honey and orange flower water and set to one side.

Put the halved nectarines on a tray and sprinkle them with the sugar, then put them under a hot grill (broiler). Cook until the nectarines are lightly golden and beginning to blister. Remove, and serve with the flavoured yoghurt.

SERVES 4

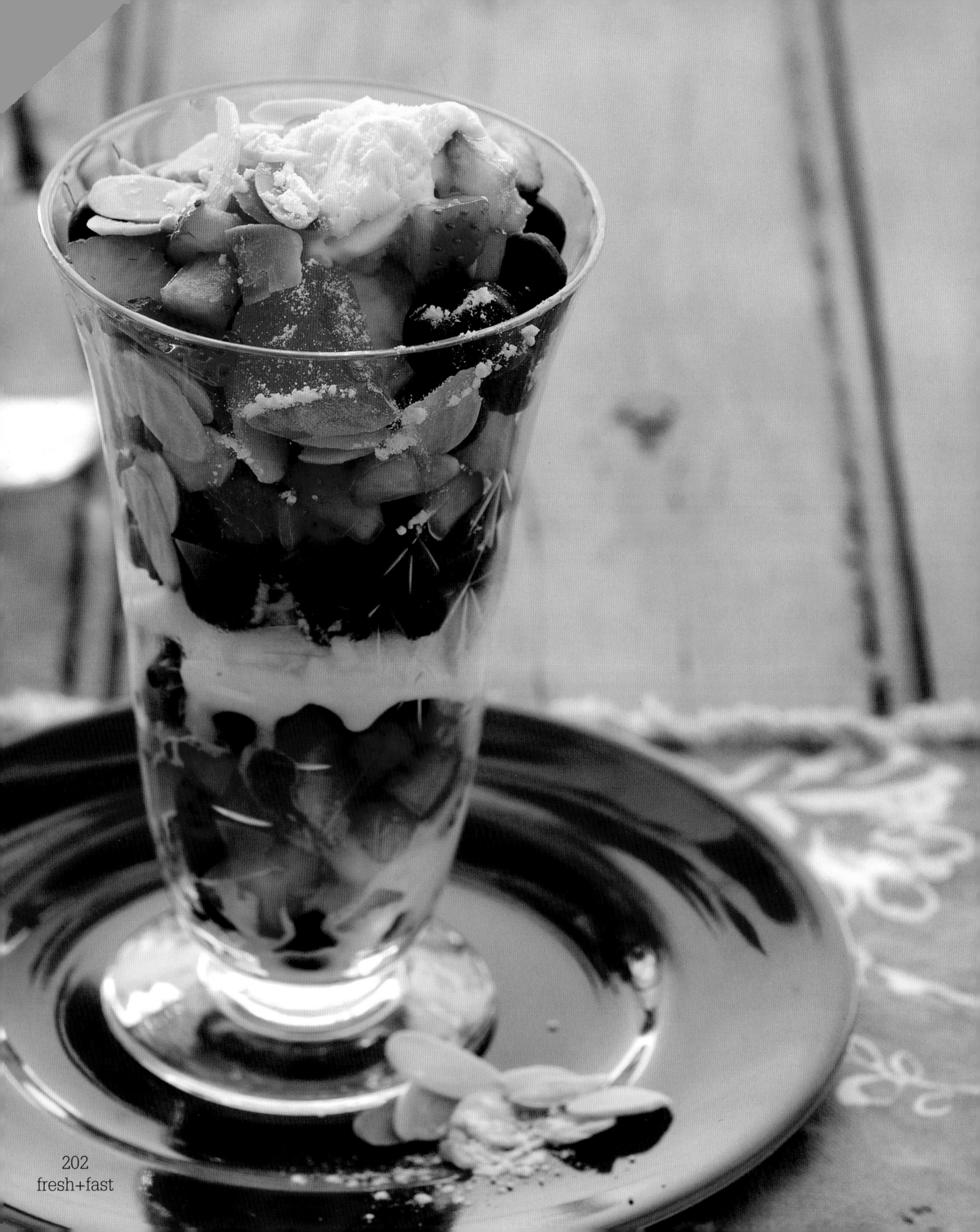

strawberry and Turkish delight sundaes

50 g (1¾ oz) flaked almonds
2 squares Turkish delight
250 g (9 oz/1⅔ cups) strawberries
150 g (5½ oz/1 cup) blueberries
300 ml (10½ fl oz) vanilla ice cream

Preheat the oven to 180°C (350°F/Gas 4).

Put the flaked almonds onto a baking tray and bake in the oven until golden brown. Remove and allow to cool.

Cut each Turkish delight square into 8 tiny cubes. Set aside.

Remove the stems from the strawberries and finely chop them into a bowl.

In chilled parfait glasses, layer the ice cream, blueberries, strawberries, Turkish delight and almonds.

SERVES 4

ginger-spiced oranges with caramel ice cream

5 oranges
2 tablespoons brown sugar
1 teaspoon finely grated fresh ginger
caramel ice cream to serve

Juice one of the oranges and put the juice in a bowl. Add the brown sugar and ginger and stir until the sugar has dissolved.

With a sharp knife, remove the skin and pith from the remaining oranges, then thinly slice them into the bowl. Allow to marinate for 10 minutes before serving with caramel ice cream.

SERVES 4

fruit salad

4 ripe peaches
150 g (5½ oz/1 cup) blueberries
2 bananas
4 passionfruit, pulp removed
juice of 2 oranges
1 tablespoon caster (superfine) sugar

Cut the peaches in half and remove the stones and skin. Slice into a bowl, then add the blueberries and bananas, cut into thick slices. Add the passionfruit pulp and cover with the orange juice and a sprinkle of the sugar. Lightly stir to just coat the fruit in the sweetened juice.

Serve with mango sorbet or vanilla ice cream.

SERVES 4

poached peaches with fresh raspberry sorbet

4 ripe peaches
225 g (8 oz/1 cup) sugar
1 vanilla bean, sliced in half lengthways
500 ml (17 fl oz/2 cups) water
100 g (3½ oz) frozen raspberries

Cut the peaches into quarters and remove the stones.

Put the sugar and vanilla bean into a deep-sided pan and add the water. Bring to the boil, stir until the sugar has dissolved, then reduce to a simmer. Add the peach quarters and cover with a lid. Simmer over a low heat for 5 minutes, then with a slotted spoon remove the peaches to a bowl. Allow the sauce to keep simmering for a further 5 minutes, then remove from the heat.

When cool, remove the skin from the peaches and pour over a little of the syrup. Reserve 60 ml (2 fl oz/¼ cup) of syrup. Cover both the reserved syrup and the peaches with plastic wrap and chill in the fridge until ready to serve.

Divide the peaches among four bowls.

Put the frozen raspberries in a blender or food processor with the chilled syrup. Blend to a smooth sorbet, then spoon over the peaches.

SERVES 4

sweet

delights and a dollop of fun

BUTTERMILK PUDDINGS WITH FRESH BERRIES
CHERRY SYLLABUB
FIGS AND STRAWBERRIES WITH SWEET CREAM
STEWED APRICOTS
MARINATED DRIED FIGS WITH CREAMED RICOTTA
PASSIONFRUIT PARFAIT WITH FRESH NECTARINES
FINE APPLE TART   MAPLE BAKED PEARS   HONEYED RHUBARB
CHRISTMAS PUDDING ICE CREAM

buttermilk puddings with fresh berries

150 ml (5 fl oz) milk
55 g (2 oz/¼ cup) caster (superfine)
    sugar
1 vanilla bean
1 tablespoon powdered gelatine (see
    Glossary, page 245)
500 ml (17 fl oz/2 cups) buttermilk
mixed berries to serve

Lightly oil six 100 ml (3½ fl oz) moulds
or teacups.

Put the milk and sugar in a small
saucepan. Slice the vanilla bean in half
lengthways and with a knife scrape away
the soft beans from the centre. Add them
to the milk along with the vanilla bean.
Heat over a low heat until the milk almost
comes to the boil, stirring to ensure the
sugar has dissolved. Remove from the heat
and discard the vanilla bean, before
sprinkling over the gelatine. Stir well to
ensure the gelatine has melted, then add
the buttermilk and whisk for 1 minute.
Pour into the prepared moulds and allow
to cool before refrigerating overnight.

To serve, turn the buttermilk puddings
out of the moulds and serve with a tumble
of fresh berries.

MAKES 6

opposite: cherry syllabub
this page: figs and strawberries
with sweet cream

cherry syllabub

350 g (12 oz/1¾ cups) bottled
    cherries
100 g (3½ oz) caster (superfine) sugar
50 ml (1½ fl oz) sherry
juice of 1 lemon
300 ml (10½ fl oz) cream, lightly
    whipped

Drain the cherries, reserving 50 ml
(1½ fl oz) of the juice. Spoon the cherries
into the bases of four parfait glasses or
serving bowls.

Combine the sugar, sherry, lemon juice and
reserved cherry juice. Stir until the sugar
has dissolved into the liquid.

Gently fold the sherry mixture into the
lightly whipped cream until just combined.
Spoon the cream over the cherries. Cover
and refrigerate until ready to serve.

SERVES 4

figs and strawberries with sweet cream

2 fresh organic eggs
250 g (9 oz) mascarpone cheese
2–3 tablespoons caster (superfine)
    sugar
1 teaspoon finely grated orange zest
2 tablespoons Grand Marnier
fresh figs and strawberries to serve

Separate each of the eggs. Whisk the
egg whites in a clean bowl until soft
peaks form.

Put the yolks, mascarpone, sugar, orange
zest and Grand Marnier in a separate
bowl and stir to combine. Lightly fold the
egg whites into the mascarpone mixture
until all the ingredients are well
combined. Serve with a pile of fresh figs
and strawberries.

SERVES 4

stewed apricots

200 g (7 oz) dried apricots
1 vanilla bean, split
600 ml (21 fl oz) water
½ teaspoon rosewater
1 tablespoon honey
45 g (1¾ oz/½ cup) flaked almonds, toasted
250 g (9 oz) thick (double/heavy) cream

Put the apricots in a saucepan with the vanilla bean and the water. Bring to the boil, then cover and simmer over a low heat for 1 hour or until the apricots have softened and begun to break up.

Remove the vanilla bean and stir in the rosewater and honey. Serve with a dollop of thick cream and a scatter of toasted almond flakes.

SERVES 4–6

marinated dried figs with creamed ricotta

150 g (5½ oz) small dried wild figs
50 g (1¾ oz) or 4 sprigs of dried muscatels
4 thick strips lemon zest
1 teaspoon honey
1 cup strong hot jasmine tea
200 g (7 oz) ricotta cheese
125 ml (4 fl oz/½ cup) cream
2 tablespoons caster (superfine) sugar

Put the figs, muscatels, lemon zest and honey in a small bowl and pour the jasmine tea over the top. Allow to marinate for an hour, stirring every so often to ensure all the fruit is covered by the tea.

Put the ricotta, cream and sugar in a food processor and blend until smooth.

Drain the liquid from the soaking fruit into a small saucepan and simmer over a low heat for 5 minutes or until it is reduced by half.

Arrange the figs and muscatels on four serving plates and drizzle with some of the soaking liquid. Serve with a big dollop of the creamed ricotta.

SERVES 4

passionfruit parfait with fresh nectarines

5 egg yolks
100 g (3½ oz) caster (superfine) sugar
3 cm (1¼ in) piece fresh ginger
2 tablespoons honey
125 g (4½ oz/½ cup) passionfruit pulp
500 ml (17 fl oz/2 cups) sour cream
fresh nectarines and passionfruit pulp
    (extra) to serve

Line an 8 x 22 cm (3¼ x 8½ in) loaf (bar) tin with baking paper.

Using a whisk or electric beaters, whisk the egg yolks and sugar in a large bowl until thick and pale.

Finely grate the ginger into a small bowl, then squeeze to remove the liquid until you have 2 teaspoons of ginger juice. Add the ginger juice to the whisked eggs along with the honey, passionfruit pulp and sour cream and lightly fold together. Spoon into the prepared tin and freeze overnight or until firm.

Turn the parfait out onto a clean surface and cut into six thick slices. Serve topped with a tumble of sliced nectarines and passionfruit pulp.

SERVES 6

fine apple tart

2 sheets frozen butter puff pastry
3–4 small green apples, peeled and cored
115 g (4 oz/½ cup) caster (superfine) sugar
3 tablespoons butter
vanilla ice cream or thick (double/heavy)
    cream, to serve

Preheat the oven to 200°C (400°F/Gas 6).

Cut the pastry into four rectangles. Put them on
a baking tray lined with baking paper. Finely slice
the apples and place them on top of the pastry in
a line of overlapping slices. Sprinkle with the sugar
and top with a few small blobs of butter.

Put the tarts in the oven and bake for 15 minutes
or until the pastry and apples are golden brown.
Serve warm with ice cream or cream.

SERVES 4

maple baked pears

4 corella pears
2 teaspoons unsalted butter, softened
2 tablespoons maple syrup

Preheat the oven to 180°C (350°F/Gas 4).

Halve the pears and with a teaspoon scoop
out the core. Place the pears skin side up
on a cutting board and with a sharp knife
take a thin slice from the top of each pear
(this will give them a flat surface to sit on).
Put the pears on a shallow baking tray skin
side down. Rub the butter over the surface
of the pears, then fill each of the hollowed
cores with the maple syrup. Cover with foil
and bake in the oven for 1 hour.

Serve with thick cream or vanilla
ice cream.

SERVES 4

honeyed rhubarb

450 g (1 lb) rhubarb
juice of 1 orange
1 tablespoon butter
4 tablespoons honey

Preheat the oven to 180°C (350°F/Gas 4).

Trim and rinse the rhubarb before cutting
it into 6 cm (2½ in) lengths. Put the
rhubarb into a glass or ceramic ovenproof
dish, then add the orange juice, butter
and honey. Cover with foil and bake for
half an hour.

Serve with berry sorbet or vanilla
ice cream.

SERVES 4

Christmas pudding ice cream

300 g (10½ oz) Christmas pudding
300 g (10½ oz) cherries, pitted and roughly chopped
3 tablespoons Kirsch
600 g (1 lb 5 oz) good quality vanilla ice cream, softened
raspberries, to serve

Line a terrine mould with baking paper or, if you'd like to make the ice cream into a pudding shape, line the base of a metal bowl with a circle of baking paper.

Break the pudding up into small pieces and put them in a bowl with the cherries and Kirsch. Toss lightly to combine.

Fold the cherry pudding mixture through the softened ice cream. Spoon into the terrine mould or bowl and cover with plastic wrap. Place in the freezer overnight. To serve, simply turn the ice cream out of the mould. Slice, and serve with raspberries.

SERVES 8–10

cheers

blend and share with friends

SUMMER MORNING   MANGO LASSI
LEMONADE   FRUIT PUNCH   MANGO DAIQUIRI
PIMMS WITH GINGER SYRUP
TROPICAL RUM BLEND

summer morning

250 ml (9 fl oz/1 cup) orange juice
160 g (5¾ oz/1 cup) chopped fresh
    pineapple
½ banana
pulp of 2 passionfruit
4 mint leaves
4 ice cubes

Blend the ingredients until smooth and
pour into two chilled glasses.

SERVES 2

mango lassi

240 g (8½ oz/¾ cup) roughly chopped
  mango
1 teaspoon honey
1 teaspoon lime juice
125 g (4½ oz/½ cup) plain yoghurt
1½ cups ice cubes

Blend all the ingredients until smooth and
pour into two chilled glasses.

SERVES 2

lemonade

2 organic lemons
220 g (7¾ oz/1 cup) sugar
125 ml (4 fl oz/½ cup) water
chilled sparkling mineral water,
    to serve

With a sharp knife remove strips of skin
from the two lemons, then juice the
lemons. Put the strips in a small saucepan
with the sugar and the water. Bring to the
boil over a high heat. Reduce the heat and
simmer for a few minutes, then remove
from the heat and allow to cool. Discard
the lemon strips and add the lemon juice.

Serve diluted to taste with the sparkling
mineral water.

SERVES 6–8 DEPENDING ON DILUTION

fruit punch

500 ml (17 fl oz/2 cups) peach nectar
200 ml (7 fl oz) dark rum
60 ml (2 fl oz/¼ cup) lime juice
3 peaches, peeled and finely sliced
75 ml (2½ fl oz) ginger syrup (see
    Store, page 241)
160 g (5¾ oz/1 cup) chopped
    pineapple
1 litre (35 fl oz/4 cups) ginger beer
    or ginger wine
fresh lime and mint to garnish

Put all the ingredients except the
garnishes in a large serving or punch
bowl and stir well. Garnish with thinly
sliced lime and mint.

SERVES 8

clockwise from top:
mango daiquiri, Pimms
with ginger syrup,
tropical rum blend

mango daiquiri

30 ml (1 fl oz) lime juice
2 teaspoons sugar
2 teaspoons Triple Sec or Cointreau
125 ml (4 fl oz/½ cup) white rum
300 g (10½ oz/1 cup) diced mango
6 ice cubes

Put all the ingredients in a blender
and blend until smooth. Pour into two
chilled glasses.

SERVES 2

Pimms with ginger syrup

125 ml (4 fl oz/½ cup) fresh
    pineapple juice
1½ tablespoons ginger syrup (see
    Store, page 241)
60 ml (2 fl oz/¼ cup) Pimms
4–5 ice cubes
60 ml (2 fl oz/¼ cup) soda water
lime and fresh pineapple to garnish

Put the pineapple juice, ginger syrup
and Pimms in a tall glass with ice. Top
with soda water and garnish with lime
and pineapple.

SERVES 1

tropical rum blend

30 ml (1 fl oz) white rum
30 ml (1 fl oz) Malibu
30 ml (1 fl oz) Midori
200 ml (7 fl oz) grapefruit juice
185 g (6½ oz) peeled and roughly
    chopped honeydew melon
ice to serve
honeydew melon wedges to garnish

Put the white rum, Malibu, Midori,
grapefruit juice and chopped honeydew
melon in a blender and blend until smooth.

Pour into two tall glasses over ice and
garnish with wedges of honeydew melon.

SERVES 2

store

essentials and must haves

While it's nice to think of fresh and fast food as a spontaneous response to what looks great in the marketplace, there are a few store cupboard essentials that you should always have close to hand. Some are staples, but others are the little extra flavours that add zing to any dish.

Invest in good quality vinegar and extra virgin olive oil, as these two ingredients will bring any simple salad to life. Fill the pantry with pasta, tinned tuna, salted capers, anchovies, couscous, tinned tomatoes, rice, maple syrup, tinned chickpeas, preserved lemon, bottled artichokes and good quality stock cubes.

If you want staples for the fridge then you can't go past bacon and parmesan cheese. These two basic ingredients can add robust flavour to a simple pasta, a little richness to a soup, some oomph to a salad or help to create a great omelette for a quick and easy late-night meal. Add fresh herbs and lemons to your fridge store, and you have the beginnings of many a great meal.

Always remember that keeping it simple is the best way to approach most meals and that sometimes the art can be in the shopping rather than the cooking!

The following pages offer a selection of basics to complement the previous recipes, and a glossary of common ingredients.

lemon mayonnaise

2 egg yolks
1 teaspoon mustard
1 tablespoon lemon juice
200 ml (7 fl oz) light olive oil

Whisk together the egg yolks, mustard and lemon juice until light and creamy. Drizzle in the olive oil a little at a time, whisking continuously until a thick mayonnaise forms. Season to taste.

MAKES ABOUT 250 ML (9 FL OZ/1 CUP)

ginger syrup

½ cup grated fresh ginger
220 g (7¾ oz/1 cup) sugar
250 ml (9 fl oz/1 cup) water

Put the ginger, sugar and water in a small saucepan and bring to the boil. Reduce the heat and simmer for 2–3 minutes. Strain into a container, cool and store in the refrigerator until ready to use.

MAKES ABOUT 250 ML (9 FL OZ/1 CUP)

pizza bases

250 g (9 oz/2 cups) Italian 00 pizza
    or bread flour
1 teaspoon sugar
¼ teaspoon sea salt
7 g (¼ oz) dried yeast
1 tablespoon extra virgin olive oil
125 ml (4 fl oz/½ cup) warm water

Put the flour, sugar, sea salt, yeast and olive oil into a large bowl and add enough warm water to form a smooth dough. Turn the dough out onto a floured surface and knead for 10 minutes. Form the dough into a ball and put it in a large bowl that has been lightly oiled. Cover with plastic wrap and leave to rise for 2 hours in a warm place. When the dough has doubled in size, punch it down and knead it again for a few minutes. Allow it to sit for 20 minutes before rolling out to shape.

MAKES 2 X 23 CM (9 IN) PIZZA BASES

pesto

3 large handfuls of basil leaves
a large handful of flat-leaf (Italian)
    parsley, roughly chopped
4 tablespoons roughly grated
    parmesan cheese
3 tablespoons pine nuts, toasted
½ garlic clove
150 ml (5 fl oz) olive oil

Put all the ingredients in a blender or food
processor and blend to a chunky paste.

MAKES ABOUT 250 G (9 OZ/1 CUP)

couscous

185 g (6½ oz/1 cup) instant couscous
1 tablespoon butter
250 ml (9fl oz/1 cup) boiling water

Put the couscous and butter in a large
bowl and the boiling water over the top.
Cover and allow to sit for 5 minutes, then
fluff up the grains with a fork. Cover again
and leave for a further 5 minutes. Season
with a little sea salt and freshly ground
black pepper, then rub the grains with your
fingertips to remove any lumps. Serve
warm or room temperature.

SERVES 4 AS A SIDE DISH

rouille

1 thick slice sourdough bread
a pinch of saffron threads
1 red capsicum (pepper), roasted and
    skin removed
¼ teaspoon paprika
2 garlic cloves, chopped
125 ml (4 fl oz/½ cup) light olive oil

Tear the bread into pieces and put it
in a bowl.

Put the saffron threads in a small saucepan
with 4 tablespoons of water and bring to
the boil. Simmer for 1 minute.

Pour the hot saffron water over the
bread. Allow it to sit for 1 minute before
putting it in a food processor or blender.
Add the capsicum flesh, paprika and garlic
and blend to form a smooth paste. Add the
olive oil in a slow drizzle until
a thick mayonnaise forms. Season with sea
salt to taste.

MAKES ABOUT 250 ML (9 FL OZ/1 CUP)

steamed white rice

200 g (7 oz/1 cup) white long-grain
    rice
435 ml (15¼ fl oz/1¾ cups) water

Rinse the rice under cold running water
for a few minutes. Put the drained rice in
a saucepan with a tight-fitting lid. Cover
with the water and add a pinch of sea
salt. Bring to the boil, then stir once to
ensure the grains have not stuck to the
base of the pan.

Cover the pan and turn the heat down
to the lowest setting. Cook the rice for
15 minutes, then take the pan off the heat
and allow the rice to sit for a further
10 minutes. Just before serving, fluff up
the grains with a fork.

SERVES 2–4 AS A SIDE DISH

mashed potato

1 kg (2 lb 4 oz) all-purpose potatoes
125 ml (4 fl oz/½ cup) milk
100 g (3½ oz) butter
pinch of ground white pepper

Peel the potatoes and cut them into
chunks. Put them in a large pot of cold
water, bring to the boil and cook for
30 minutes or until cooked through.

Meanwhile, put the milk and butter in a
small saucepan. Warm over a low heat
until the butter has melted.

Drain the potatoes and return to the warm
pot. Mash the potatoes while they are still
warm, then add in the buttery milk and stir
until the potato is soft and creamy. Season
with sea salt and white pepper.

SERVES 4–6 AS A SIDE DISH

lemon vinaigrette

1 tablespoon lemon juice
3 tablespoons extra virgin olive oil
1 garlic clove, bruised
½ teaspoon honey

Put all the ingredients in a small screw-top
jar and shake. Season to taste and shake
again just before drizzling over salads.

MAKES ABOUT 80 ML (2½ FL OZ/⅓ CUP)

glossary

balsamic vinegar

Balsamic vinegar is a dark, fragrant, sweetish aged vinegar made from grape juice. The production of authentic balsamic vinegar is carefully controlled. Bottles of the real thing are labelled Aceto Balsamico Tradizionale de Modena, while commercial varieties simply have Aceto Balsamico de Modena. Caramelised balsamic vinegar is a sweetened reduction that is thicker, sweeter and less acidic than regular balsamic vinegar and is available from most speciality food stores.

bocconcini cheese

These are small balls of fresh mozzarella cheese, often sold sitting in their own whey. When fresh they are soft and springy to the touch and have a milky taste. They are available from delicatessens.

buffalo mozzarella

A soft, creamy white mozzarella cheese traditionally made in southern Italy. It is considered to be the best quality mozzarella due to its texture and flavour.

burghul

Popular in the Middle East, burghul (bulgur) is the key ingredient in tabouleh and pilaff. You can buy these wheat kernels either whole or cracked into fine, medium or coarse grains. They are pre-steamed and pre-baked to minimise cooking time.

butter puff pastry

This is made with butter rather than vegetable fat, which gives it a much more buttery flavour than standard puff pastry. If you can't find any, brush ordinary puff pastry with melted butter to add flavour.

buttermilk

This low-fat dairy product is made from skim milk and milk powder, using a culture similar to yoghurt. It is often used in baking (as a raising agent) and can be found in the refrigerated section of most supermarkets.

cannellini beans

These small white beans are most commonly used in soups, stews and salads. They can be bought dried, or pre-cooked in tins.

casarecci

These short lengths of rolled and twisted Italian pasta are traditionally served with a meat sauce. This style of pasta is now commercially produced and is available in most large supermarkets.

Chinese roasted duck

These whole ducks are rubbed with Chinese spices, then roasted until the skin is crispy and a glossy, golden brown. You can buy them freshly cooked from speciality Chinese stores and butchers.

chocolate

Couverture is the best-quality chocolate. This bittersweet chocolate contains the highest percentage of cocoa butter and is sold in good delicatessens and food stores. If you are unable to obtain chocolate of this standard, it is preferable to use good quality eating chocolate rather than cheap cooking chocolate. Cooking chocolates, on the whole, do not have a good flavour and tend to result in an oily rather than buttery texture.

couscous

Couscous is the favoured dish of North Africa. It is made from a flour-coated granular semolina and traditionally steamed in a couscousiere. Nowadays, instant couscous is available in most large supermarkets.

dried Asian fried shallots

Crisp-fried shallots or onions are available from most Asian grocery stores and are normally packaged in plastic tubs or bags. They are used as a flavour enhancer, scattered over rice and savoury dishes.

fish sauce

This pungent liquid made from fermented fish is widely used in South-East Asian cooking to add a salty, savoury flavour. Buy a small bottle and store it in the fridge.

garam masala

This popular Indian spice blend features ground cumin, coriander, cardamom, cloves and nutmeg.

gelatine

Leaf gelatine is available in sheets of varying sizes. Always check the manufacturer's instructions regarding which ratio of liquid to gelatine sheet to use. If leaves are unavailable, use gelatine powder instead, making sure it is well dissolved in warm liquid before using in recipes. Again, refer to the manufacturer's instructions.

hoisin sauce

A Chinese sauce made from a base of fermented soya beans. Hoisin has a distinctive salty, sweet flavour with a hint of garlic and Chinese five-spice.

kecap manis

This is a thick, sweet-flavoured soy sauce used in Indonesian cooking.

lemongrass

These long, fragrant stems are very popular in Thai cuisine. The tough outer layers should be stripped off first, and the white stem can then be used either finely chopped or whole in soups. Lemongrass will keep refrigerated for up to 2 weeks.

mascarpone cheese

This heavy, Italian-style set cream is used as a base in many sweet and savoury dishes. It is made from cream rather than milk, so is high in fat. A popular use is in the Italian dessert tiramisu. It is sold in delicatessens and supermarkets.

mirin

Mirin is a rice wine used in Japanese cooking. It adds sweetness to sauces and dressings, and is used for marinating and glazing dishes such as teriyaki. It is available from Asian grocery stores and most supermarkets.

niçoise olives

Niçoise or Ligurian olives are small black olives that are often used in salads or scattered over prepared dishes. They are not suitable for making into pastes (tapenades).

orange flower water

This perfumed distillation of bitter-orange blossoms is mostly used as a flavouring in baked goods and drinks. It is sold in large supermarkets and delicatessens.

orzo

This small rice-shaped pasta is often used in soups.

palm sugar

Palm sugar, also known as jaggery, is obtained from the sap of various palm trees and is sold as hard cakes, or in cylinders and in plastic jars. If it is very hard it will need to be grated. It can be found in Asian grocery stores or large supermarkets. Substitute dark brown sugar when palm sugar is unavailable.

panettone

An aromatic northern Italian yeast bread made with raisins and candied peel, panettone is traditionally eaten at Christmas, when it is sold in Italian delicatessens or large supermarkets. It is available in large and small sizes.

papaya

This large tropical fruit can be red, orange or yellow. It contains an enzyme that stops gelatine setting, so avoid using it in jellies. It is sometimes called a pawpaw, but is really part of the custard apple family. Green papayas, often used in Asian cooking, can be bought from specialty Asian food stores.

passata

A rich, thick tomato purée made from sieved tomatoes. It can be used as a base in sauces and soups.

polenta

Polenta is a yellow, grainy cornmeal that is slowly cooked in boiling water to form a thick, savoury porridge.

pomegranate molasses

This is a thick syrup made from the reduction of pomegranate juice. It has a bittersweet flavour, which adds a sour bite to many Middle Eastern dishes. It is available from Middle Eastern speciality stores. The closest substitute is sweetened tamarind.

preserved lemon

These are whole lemons preserved in salt or brine, which turns their rind soft and pliable. Only the rind is used in cooking—the pulp should be scraped out and discarded. The lemons are available from delicatessens and large supermarkets.

prosciutto

Prosciutto or Parma ham is a lightly salted, air-dried ham. It is commonly sold in paper-thin slices, and can be found in most large supermarkets and delicatessens.

puy lentils

Originally grown in the volcanic soils of the Puy region in France, these lentils are highly prized for their flavour and the fact that they hold their shape during cooking.

rice wine vinegar

Made from fermented rice, this vinegar comes in clear, red and black versions. If no colour is specified in a recipe, use the clear vinegar. The clear rice wine vinegar is sweeter and milder than its European counterparts or the darker and sharper-flavoured Chinese black vinegar.

risoni

Risoni are small rice-shaped pasta. They are ideal for use in soups or salads where their small shape is able to absorb the other flavours in the dish.

rosewater

The distilled essence of rose petals, rosewater is used in small quantities to impart a perfumed flavour to pastries, fruit salads and sweet puddings. It is available from delicatessens and large supermarkets.

saffron threads

The orange-red stigmas from one species of crocus plant, saffron threads are the most expensive spice in the world. Each flower consists of three stigmas, which are hand-picked, then dried—a very labour-intensive process. Saffron should be bought in small quantities and used sparingly as it has a very strong flavour. Beware of inexpensive brands when buying saffron, as cheap 'real' saffron does not exist!

salted capers

These are the green buds from a Mediterranean shrub, preserved in brine or salt. Salted capers have a firmer texture and are often smaller than those preserved in brine. Rinse away the saltiness before using them. Available from good delicatessens.

sashimi-grade fish

Fish sold for making sushi and sashimi is intended to be eaten raw, and so is usually the freshest fish at the markets. Buy a thick piece cut from the centre rather than the narrower tail end.

smoked paprika

Paprika is commonly sold as a dried, rich-red powder made from a member of the chilli family. It is sold in many grades, from delicate through to sweet and finally hot. Smoked paprika from Spain adds a distinct rich, smoky flavour to recipes and is well worth looking for if you enjoy introducing these flavours into your favourite dishes.

soba noodles

These thin buckwheat noodles are an ideal base for many Asian-style noodle salads or soups. They are usually sold dried and are sometimes flavoured with green tea.

sour cherries

Sour or morello cherries are commonly sold bottled in sweet juice and are available from most supermarkets. They have a slightly tart flavour, and are ideal for baking.

sourdough bread

Sourdough is a French-style bread that uses a fermented dough as its raising agent. It is commonly sold as a thick-textured country-style loaf.

star anise

This pretty, star-shaped dried fruit contains small, oval, brown seeds. Star anise has a flavour similar to aniseed, but is more liquorice-like. It is commonly used whole because of its decorative shape.

stracchino cheese

A soft, fresh cow's milk cheese with a velvety white rind which is a specialty of the Lombardy region. It can be eaten fresh with bread or sliced over pizza. Substitute with Taleggio or fresh mozzarella.

sumac

Sumac is a peppery, sour spice made from dried and ground sumac berries. The fruit of a shrub found in the northern hemisphere, it is widely used in Middle Eastern cookery. Sumac is available from most large supermarkets and Middle Eastern speciality stores.

tamarind

Tamarind is the sour pulp of an Asian fruit. It is most commonly available compressed into cakes or refined as tamarind concentrate in jars. Tamarind concentrate is widely available; the pulp can be found in Asian food shops.

tofu

This white curd is made from soya beans and is a good source of protein. Bland in taste, it takes on the flavour of other ingredients. Tofu is usually sold in blocks and comes in several different grades— soft (silken), firm, sheets and deep-fried. Refrigerate fresh tofu covered in water for up to 5 days, changing the water daily.

vanilla bean

The long, slim, black vanilla bean has a caramel aroma synthetic vanillas can never capture. Good quality beans are soft and not too dry. Store unused vanilla pods in a full jar of caster (superfine) sugar—this will help keep the vanilla fresh, and the aroma of the bean will quickly infuse the sugar, making it a wonderful addition to desserts and baking.

vanilla essence

When using vanilla essence, always ensure it is made from real vanilla and is not labelled 'imitation' vanilla extract or essence. The flavours are quite different, with the imitation being almost acrid in its aftertaste. See also vanilla bean.

vine leaves

The large, green leaves of the grapevine are sold packed in tins, jars or plastic packs or in brine. They are used in Greek and Middle Eastern cookery to wrap foods for cooking. Vine leaves in brine should be rinsed before use to remove some of the salty flavour. Before using fresh young vine leaves, simmer them in water for 10 minutes to soften them.

wasabi

Mostly sold in tubes or in a powdered dried form (mixed to a paste with a little water), wasabi comes from the dark green root of a Japanese aquatic plant and has a very hot flavour. It is used to flavour sushi, sashimi and some sauces.

index

This book may be titled fresh + fast but the process involved in creating such a book is never fast or easy. All the people involved in its production have offered their talent and advice generously and I offer a warm thank-you.

I'd like to start with Murdoch books, and in particular Kay Scarlett and Juliet Rogers for allowing me to work on the marie claire series. Thank you once again.

The team in the test kitchen did a fantastic job of testing the recipes and making queries whenever it was necessary. Thanks to all, for your honesty and assistance.

Desney Shoemark has done an amazing job of pulling together the multitude of threads that started in a jumble at the beginning of the book and which have now united into a single piece. She has calmly harassed me when necessary with humour and soothing words. Thank you so much for keeping myself, and the book, on course.

This is a book of food and life and it's essence has been captured by two wonderful photographers. Anthony Ong celebrates the joy of sunny days spent with friends in his gorgeous images of Tegan, Rebecca and Stephanie. Thank you for the sunshine. Gorta Yuuki brought his quiet humour and his calm serenity to the studio. Thank you for bringing the food to life.

Heidi Flett was the angel in the kitchen. A heartfelt thanks for your cheering laughs, helpful suggestions, yummy food and friendship.

When we started this book we wanted a new vision for the marie claire series. Gayna Murphy has provided that vision with a new look and a beautifully designed book. Thank you so much for all the hard work and generosity that was necessary to manifest and maintain that vision.

There are always those behind-the-scenes people who smooth the way and enhance the process. In particular, I'd like to thank Tony Gilding of Byron Plantation for making the location shoot such a pleasant experience for the team, as well as Jack and Yvonne Harper for the use of their farm and fresh produce. Thanks also to Vivien Valk and Jane Lawson of Murdoch Books for wise words, helpful insights and their clear overview.

I'd like to thank my family of boys who provide me with humour and hugs, love and laughter on a daily basis despite the fact that 'the book' often takes over my life.

Thank you for everything.

Published in 2008 by Murdoch Books

Murdoch Books Australia
83 Alexander Street
Crows Nest NSW 2065
Phone: +61 (0) 2 8425 0100
Fax: +61 (0) 2 9906 2218
www.murdochbooks.com.au

Murdoch Books UK
Erico House, 6th Floor
93–99 Upper Richmond Road
Putney, London SW15 2TG
Phone: +44 (0) 20 8785 5995
Fax: +44 (0) 20 8785 5985
www.murdochbooks.co.uk

Chief executive: Juliet Rogers
Publishing director: Kay Scarlett

Project manager and editor: Desney Shoemark
Design concept, art direction and design: Gayna Murphy
Stylists: Michele Cranston (food), Gayna Murphy (lifestyle and food) and Caterina Scardino (fashion)
Photographers: Anthony Ong (fashion and lifestyle) and Gorta Yuuki (food)
Food preparation: Heidi Flett
Models: Stephanie Eales, Tegan Findlay and Rebecca Seidel from Chic
Hair and make-up: Katrina Raftery from Viviens
Production: Kita George

National Library of Australia Cataloguing-in-Publication Data

Cranston, Michele.
Marie Claire fresh and fast / Michele Cranston.
Sydney : Murdoch Books, 2008.
ISBN 9781741962338 (pbk.)
Includes index.
Cookery (Natural foods) Quick and easy cookery.
Marie Claire (North Sydney, N.S.W.)
641.5

A catalogue record for this book is available from the British Library.

Colour separation by Splitting Image Colour Studio, Melbourne, Australia.
Printed by 1010 Printing International Limited in 2008. PRINTED IN CHINA. Reprinted 2010 (three times), 2013.

The Publisher and stylists would like to thank Emmanuelle Flahault from Nell Design for lending her beautiful textiles,
and Planet Furniture, for lending some of the other items used in photography within the book.

IMPORTANT: Those who might be at risk from the effects of salmonella poisoning (the elderly, pregnant women,
young children and those suffering from immune deficiency diseases) should consult their doctor with any concerns
about eating raw eggs.

CONVERSION GUIDE: You may find cooking times vary depending on the oven you are using. For fan-forced ovens,
as a general rule, set the oven temperature to 20°C (35°F) lower than indicated in the recipe. We have used 20 ml
(4 teaspoon) tablespoon measures. If you are using a 15 ml (3 teaspoon) tablespoon, for most recipes the difference
will not be noticeable. However, for recipes using baking powder, gelatine, bicarbonate of soda (baking soda), small
amounts of flour and cornflour (cornstarch), add an extra teaspoon for each tablespoon specified.